THE COMPLETE GUIDE TO
TOTAL
TRANSFORMATION

Be the Hero of Your Own Life Story,
Fulfill Your Purpose, Master Your Destiny

The international best-selling online course,
now available as a book!

Joeel A. Rivera, M.Ed.
& Natalie Rivera

ISBN 978-1-60166-053-4

FREE ONLINE COURSE!

*Flip to the end of this book to find out how to enroll in the
FREE online course that bring this book to life!*

Plus, learn how to become a Transformation Life Coach.

TRANSFORMATION
— PUBLISHING —

CONTENTS

SECTION 1: TRANSFORMATION

1: ANSWERING THE CALL

Have you heard the call of your true self, reminding you of your forgotten dreams?

Have you felt drawn to break free of your limitations and live more authentically?

Is there a fire within you that burns fiercely even after years of trying to snuff it out?

Have wake-up calls and ah-ha moments inspired you to finally embrace becoming who you were meant to be?

Transformation happens.

Sometimes it sneaks up on us after years of quiet suffering. Other times it is the inevitable side effect of a life struck by a sudden tsunami of unwanted change and pain. Sometimes we dive head-first into the journey we feel called to, but other times we cling desperately to "what was", like a terrified butterfly unwilling to let go of the empty casing that once housed the caterpillar. Life is exhausting, painful, and dark when trapped in the cell of our resistance to change.

The truth is we cannot always control what happens in our lives, but we can control what we do with it. We have a choice—we can submit to a life of mediocrity and unfulfillment, or we can decide that life is supposed to be more—that we have a greater purpose for being here and we will do whatever it takes to determine our own destiny.

We invite you embark on a quest—a hero's journey. Along the way, you'll no longer see your pain or challenges as obstacles, but instead you'll see them as steppingstones to a greater purpose. You'll stop allowing others to write the chapters of your life story, and you'll decide, once and for all, to live life on your terms.

Transformation is an inside job, and change is a process. This book isn't just a list of processes to create lasting change and reach your goals, although it does cover that. This book is about changing from the inside out and preventing the obstacles that tend to stop people from reaching their true potential.

And that's why this book is designed to help you:

- Identify the blocks that hold you back so you can become unstoppable
- Overcome fear of change, rejection and failure so you can feel confident going for your dream
- Develop self-mastery by reprogramming limiting beliefs
- Develop a growth mindset so you know without a doubt that nothing can stand in your way again
- Get absolutely clear about what you REALLY want and who you REALLY are so you can stop living everyone else's dreams

We invite you to join us on a quest of transformation that will lead you on a hero's journey to a place where you really can do what you dream of and become all that you are meant to be.

So, will you answer the call?

2: TRANSFORMATION IS AN INSIDE JOB, CHANGE IS A PROCESS

Nothing in life stands still. Change is constant, inevitable. Science has shown us that the entire human body—every cell—completely regenerates itself within a span of about seven years. Brain scientists and psychologists have agreed that in each moment our brains are taking in new information and our minds are constantly assimilating this information into our neural network of thoughts, beliefs, and associations.

You cannot have a new experience without it literally changing your mind, and life cannot exist without continuous growth and expansion. You are actually changing as you read these words. You are moving, growing, expanding, and changing. It is no secret that the world around you is constantly changing as well.

There is no question: You are changing. The wonderful thing about this "human experience" is that you have the power and ability to direct changes in your life. In fact, what you feel, think, say, and believe about your life is constantly putting change into motion, regardless of whether you realize it or not. You are creating your life as you go along, so you might as well create it intentionally. All that is required is a choice.

YOU ARE AT A CHOICE POINT. You can choose to continue on with your life as you currently are living it, letting the external world and your past dictate what you experience, or you can choose to create your life to be everything that you dream.

This being the case you would think we humans might be more accustomed to the change process. Instead we often live in resistance, or even fierce opposition, to change, and therefore to life itself. We often sabotage our efforts to change because we fear that if we change, we'll lose something. Our friends. Our security. Our identity. And so, making intentional change is a process. It involves identifying what we want, anticipating mental and practical obstacles, and creating action plans to get there. It can be challenging, but it's a process that can be learned and practiced.

But transformation is different. Transformation is an inside job. Someone might change their job, change their relationship, or change their hair. But when someone transforms, everything changes. They don't just make changes in their life circumstances, they dismantle the limiting beliefs that lead to the undesirable circumstances in the first place. They don't change an aspect of their life, they change the way they live their life—the way they think and feel—they change their identity—who they are.

When someone transforms, often the changes they had been putting off happen naturally. It's easier to make difficult changes when WHO YOU ARE is no longer a match for the life you are leaving behind.

And so, in this book, we're going to explore everything it takes to transform from within. We'll explore everything from identity to the hero's journey, and from limiting beliefs to developing a growth mindset. And we'll also address the process of creating lasting change, including identifying what you really want, anticipating obstacles, and creating concrete action plans.

But, primarily, this book isn't about making changes. It's about BE-ING the change. It's about becoming who you really are so you can make your unique impact on the world.

3: WHAT HOLDS PEOPLE BACK FROM CREATING LASTING CHANGE

Even when faced with a life-threatening situation, people tend to re-sist change despite knowing the repercussions. Studies reveal that when heart disease patients who had undergone traumatic bypass surgery were told if they did not adjust their lifestyle they would die, or at best undergo the life-saving procedure again, only 9% modified their behavior.

We're going to go over the internal and external obstacles that tend to hold people back from creating transformational change. These problems can prevent a person from ever reaching out to a coach, however even with a coach these issues can derail a person's progress. That's why it is important for a transformation coach to understand how and why these problems arise and what to do about them.

Why do people find it so hard to change even when they know it's good for them? There are some important biological reasons for this.

First, even bad habits are rewarding: The brain values efficiency and when something becomes habituated, the brain can go on autopilot, allowing it to significantly reduce its expenditure of energy. As a way of encouraging the person to habituate most things in life, the brain is de-signed to reward habituation, sameness, and routine by giving a burst of feel-good chemicals. The familiar feels good, even if it is obviously bad for you. This is why it is so difficult to stop smoking. It is not the physi-cal addiction to the nicotine that has proven hardest to overcome, it is the habit of the behavior of smoking that makes it so hard to kick.

The brain's programming: Our brains are wired with an error alert system that used to serve us well when a new sound in the bush could mean certain death. Our brains are hyper-vigilant to identify possible threats, con-stantly trying to protect us from harm. To the brain anything outside of the ordinary or new---aka an error—serves as an alert that something is wrong and action must be taken to avoid this new thing. This is why change is inherently hard. Although we know that it is required for what we want to occur, our brain fights us because it sees the new experiences as a threat, causing anxiety and fear in an attempt at stopping us from moving forward.

Add to that the fact that our brain rewards us for avoiding a threat. When we back down from a confrontation, a threat has been diverted, or something we find scary (like giving a presentation) comes to an end, we feel a rush of dopamine—a sense of relief—that rewards us for keeping ourselves safe. For that reason, when we face the fears of change our brains are trying their best to get us to give in to the desire for relief—to make the threat go away—to stop the change from coming.

Obviously, most humans do not live in a perilous environment in which we are threatened to the point of actual survival anymore. However, we're still stuck with the brains we have evolved to have, including their programming. But, the good news is awareness of these tendencies gives us the ability to stop the automatic reactions and take control of our lives.

Because of our programming, there are several specific obstacles that can get in the way of deliberate change.

- **Fear of Rejection/Judgment/Being Different:** This is ultimately the need for approval.
- **Fear of Uncertainty/Discomfort:** We are hard-wired to seek comfort and certainty, and avoid failure.
- **Stuck in Habits/Patterns:** We are creatures of habit who value routine.
- **Overwhelm:** The tendency to suffer from disorganization, lack of clarity, and catastrophic thinking.
- **Confidence and Self-efficacy:** The lack in belief in their abilities or inability to trust themselves.
- **Fear of Disappointment/Failure:** Lack of faith that it will work out and fear of not meeting our own expectations, or others not meeting our expectations.
- **Fear of Unintended Consequences:** Change begets change. When one area of life is changed, it impacts other areas. Sometimes it requires other changes, and those changes may be scary or unpleasant. Sometimes changes impact other people and it can be hard and emotional straining to handle their reaction.
- **Lack of Clarity/Motivation:** The tendency for people not to know what they want or why they want it.

Ask yourself, which of these reasons tend to hold you back?

Notes

SECTION 2: LET THE JOURNEY BEGIN

1: THE BUTTERFLY: A STORY OF TRANSFORMATION

(A story from Natalie.) The butterfly is a symbol that represents the process of human transformation. A caterpillar goes about its life believing that the reality it exists in is all there is. It has no idea of its true potential. It has no idea that one day it will fly. This is how life unfolds for most people. They get so wrapped up in their everyday lives that they come to believe it is all there is. They don't know their true potential. But, unlike caterpillars, humans have a higher level of awareness. They see butterflies and know that they were once a caterpillar. They have dreams of flying but they don't know how and so submit to life on the ground.

But the caterpillar feels a calling… to turn inward… to cocoon itself… to change somehow. Humans feel this call too… it's an ache in our hearts for forgotten dreams… an impulse to do something different, radical… a fire within us that no matter how hard we try to stuff it down still burns. And when we don't answer this call, often life sends us wake-up calls. Who we truly are at our deepest core will stop at nothing to break free. We start to pay attention to how we feel. We ask ourselves the deeper questions—about what it all means, what this life is for, and who we truly are. And as we reach a tipping point of personal awareness and self-determination we enter a chrysalis and the transformation begins.

Transformation is an inside job. It isn't always pretty or easy, but it always leads us to a life of meaning and authenticity. Here is my transformation story.

When a caterpillar approaches its time of transformation, it begins to eat ravenously, consuming everything in sight. The caterpillar outgrows its own skin many times, until it is too bloated to move. It turns its world on its head as it attaches itself upside-down to a branch and forms a chrysalis. This gentle encasing limits its freedom and protects it during the duration of the metamorphosis.

I can totally relate to this process. At one point in my life, I began ravenously consuming every inspirational book in sight. I felt heavy and as if I'd outgrown my life, yet I couldn't move. My world turned upside down. I felt like I was in a prison. Unbeknown to me, I was preparing for a period of personal transformation. I had been living a stagnant life for a decade, dwelling in my comfort zone of detachment and security. Everything was as I had always known it. Life was relatively easy. Simple. No drama. I'd been tolerating what was labeled as "chronic fatigue syndrome" for more than 10 years, so low energy was my norm. If you had asked me at the time I would have said I was happy, but isolation within my family, self-sheltering, and denial can create that effect.

Don't get me wrong, I had some amazing times, a fantastic best friend who kept me sane, and I spent a lot of time with family. Yet I woke up every morning to my alarm clock and contemplated all the evil things I would be willing to do if I would NEVER have to hear that damn thing again. Even though I liked my coworkers and didn't mind my job, I loathed the whole working process. I felt like a voluntary slave. I had always told myself it was what I HAD to do—everyone else had to work too, after all. I had an empty, almost non-existent marriage, yet I was totally oblivious to it. I had convinced myself that feeling unfulfilled, lonely, and unloved was pretty "normal" and that having no conflict meant I was doing better than average. My conscious mind had submitted to a life of servitude and mediocrity, but my unconscious mind and my Soul knew deeply that I was so much more.

It's as if my true self was conspiring to shift my reality. I reached a point where didn't know what would happen if I answered my call to different life, but I knew I could no longer live a life that wasn't mine. I let go and embraced my impending chrysalis and my fate. Little did I know just how quickly metamorphosis takes place.

Once inside the cocoon, the caterpillar does not reorganize its parts and sprout wings. It disintegrates into a puddle of ooze. If we were to open the cocoon halfway through the process, we would not find a cater-pillar-butterfly hybrid, instead there would be a blob of goo. A common misperception is that the cells of the caterpillar rearrange into the but-terfly; however, recent discoveries have unveiled the mind-boggling truth. Within this ooze, a new type of cells that scientists refer to as "imaginal cells" begin to form, as if from thin air. They resonate at a different fre-quency and are so totally different from the caterpillar cells that its im-mune system thinks they are enemies and gobbles them up!

Eventually the imaginal cells become so numerous that the caterpil-lar's immune system cannot destroy them fast enough. Like attracts like, and so the imaginal cells are drawn together and begin forming clumps that then cluster together and feed off the caterpillar soup in which they are developing. As if by magic, one day the imaginal cells collectively become conscious of the what they are creating—an entirely new organ-ism—and so they begin taking on different roles and creating the intricate workings of a butterfly.

During my metamorphosis, my life disintegrated completely. Every-thing that no longer served me (which was nearly everything) began to fall away, rapidly. It was sticky and messy and at times I felt like I was being torn apart, but at the same time I felt as if evolution had taken me over and I knew with every fiber of my being that I was on the right path. Within six months there was no trace of anything that had been in my life before. I walked away from my job. I sold my house. I ended my marriage. I disconnected from people who drained me of life. I sold my belongings. I found a new home for my dog. I was unrecognizable and identity-less. I was neither bloated caterpillar nor emerging butterfly, just a blob of primordial ooze, ripe with infinite possibilities!

Each new spark of imagination and inspiration ignited a flame of knowing within me, an awareness that I was changing. As I embraced who I really was, circumstances that didn't serve me shifted away with greater speed, and I was drawn to live in alignment with my true self, my passions, my talents, and my longings with greater intensity.

When the butterfly has matured, the chrysalis becomes transparent. The need for restriction has been outgrown. The butterfly emerges upside down and holds onto the empty shell with such reverence, as if to say "thank you" to where it came from.

Suddenly things became clear to me. I was ready, and so I emerged back into the world, totally transformed. For a while I dangled uncomfortably, in shock at what had happened and who I had become. I felt vulnerable, crinkled, and damp after breaking free from my womb of change. I clung to the remnants for a little while as I took deep breaths and learned to stretch my wings. I was in awe and appreciation for all that I'd been through—the emptiness, the depression, the numbness, the inspiration, the transmutation, and the reemerging. I didn't know what to do next but trusted that when it was time, the wind would gently nudge me to let go and ride the currents of my new life. I was not afraid—nothing had ever felt so right.

I was authentically, totally, and emphatically ME for the first time in my life.

I took one last look back at all that I had been and then released it completely. I was blown away at how effortless it is to fly when you allow yourself to be who you truly are. Instantaneously everything I needed for my new life was drawn to me, one after another. A relationship that fulfilled my longing for true love and acted as a catalyst for my expansion entered my life, as did living environments within which I could get acquainted with my new self. As I came into alignment with ME, I became aware that there was a larger transformation taking place. There were countless others experiencing similar episodes of metamorphosis, and somehow I "knew" that we were all part of something much greater.

I became aware that I was not alone. I felt drawn to other people who were willing to take radical personal responsibility and risk the pain and fear of total transformation in order to live life on their terms and fulfill their life's greater purpose. If you are hearing these words, you are one of these people. Whether you're a caterpillar looking longingly at the butterflies flying above you or you're clinging to the remnants of the life you know is no longer yours, your job is to answer the call. Trust the process. Embrace who you truly are. Doing so gives others permission to do the same. A revolution of transformation and awakening starts with you.

2: REWRITING YOUR STORY

(A story from Joeel.) When I look back at my life, I barely recognize the person that I was. I've transformed so much (my environment, my thought process, my belief system) that I feel like I'm a completely dif-

ferent person that lives in a completely different reality. Here I will share several elements of my story, emphasizing the ways in which my life changed as I changed my story.

Moving Constantly

In early elementary school, I moved from Puerto Rico to Florida, USA with my mom, when my parents got divorced. From that point forward, my mom moved every year or so. I went to many different elementary schools, middle and high schools. I hated the fact that I would make friends and then move again, starting over in a new school, being the new kid, and having to make new friends, again.

As I became a teenager, I started looking at the constant moving in a different way. I started seeing the positives of it. Every time I moved there was a new beginning. Every time I moved I would meet new people. I learned that even within the United States, every place I moved had a totally different culture. In each new place I was learning about different belief systems and ways of living. It opened my reality to a different world. So, with this new perspective, I started embracing change, getting to the point that I actually started to like moving.

Interestingly, as an adult I continued the pattern of frequent moving and the story I had told myself about the positive benefits of it. Even though I now had full control over where I lived, every year I would move. If I didn't move, I started getting restless. Many years later I recognized this pattern and started questioning, "is moving all the time truly what I want?" The truth is I hated having to spend all that time and energy looking for a new place to move, packing, moving, unpacking and the disruption to all of my routines. I asked myself, "do I want something more stable?" When I reflected, I realized that I didn't want to move as regularly. Although I did enjoy the novelty, I was no longer willing to continue disrupting my life. I realized it was part of my story that I wanted to change.

Not College Material

Despite the continuous changing of schools as a child, I did well as a student, even into high school. However, after a move to Tennessee, USA in the middle of high school, moving away from my girlfriend and facing being the only Hispanic student, and the resulting racism, I became tired of it. I decided to move to Puerto Rico to finish out my education while living with my dad. I was angry and resentful about many things, and found myself having to prove myself in this new environment. The circle of friends that I surrounded myself was running the streets, where it was a common occurrence to attend funerals of other youth who did not survive the environment. My grades suffered and I got myself in my share of trouble. I was told repeatedly that I was not college material.

So, when I decided that I was going to college to study marine biology, some people laughed at me, including teachers and family. When my father flew me to Pennsylvania for my first day college, the first thing that happened is that my advisor called the Dean of the college over to meet me. He looked at me and my father and said, "you called me over here for *this*?" and walked away.

I was soon to learn that the Dean was not the only person who was not pleased to be meeting a Hispanic student.

As one of the only minorities in the school, I wasn't accepted by my fellow students or my teachers. My teachers planted seeds of doubt before I'd even turned in my first paper, asking me if I was college material. Even though I am a non-violent person by nature, I was constantly having to use aggression to stand my ground against my classmates. They even wrote "go home spic" in the snow outside my window. My dorm room was routinely ransacked and searched, as they suspected me of selling drugs. I was even handcuffed and knocked unconscious by a police officer when I hadn't done anything wrong.

Eventually the expectations and opinions of others worked their way into my psyche. I became who they expected me to be. I solidified the belief system that I wasn't smart enough or capable enough. I wasn't college material.

I failed my first year of college.

Finding Purpose in Death

I returned to Puerto Rico, feeling like a failure, and continued down a dark path. I just started to give up on my dreams. I went to work in construction. A couple months later, life sent me a wake-up call.

My little brother passed away in a car accident. His death was the most painful thing that I ever experienced. Not only was he my best friend, he also followed in my footsteps. It was his irresponsible behavior and driving, that he learned from me, that lead to his death.

But something happened to me that changed my life forever. It changed my story. I had always looked at him as somebody that was immortal—nthing could ever happen to him. Him and I did many crazy things together and we were always fine. Him dying made me realize the vulnerability of life. I started questioning whether I was wrong about my own ability to survive the way we were living.

What else am I wrong about? What is possible in life? I have to embrace life now because who knows what tomorrow brings?

I took that pain and created purpose out of it, but it didn't happen overnight. I was a mess. I couldn't sleep and I would pass out during the day from high blood pressure. I decided to move to Florida to live with my mom, in order to change my environment and enroll in a community college and try again. But, the environment followed me and I found myself lost. After several months of mourning life gave me a second chance.

A police officer pulled me over after I had been underaged drinking. As I waited for him to come to my window, I grabbed the crucifix that my brother was wearing when he passed away and I said to my brother, out loud, "if you get me out of this one I will change". I talked to the officer, as I stood in handcuffs. I told them, "If you arrest me I will lose my scholarship. If you give me the opportunity, I will change my life." I begged and pleaded with them. To my surprise he drove me home and told me he was giving me one last chance. That night I had dream where I saw and talked to my brother.

When I woke up, I was determined to give his name a purpose. I had a vision to open a center to help youth who went through what we went through growing up. Again, I faced many who doubted I could do it. But this time I knew I could, I WOULD, because I had a higher calling.

I returned to school and that first semester I took a psychology class that changed my understanding of my myself, my mind, and my life. My psychology professor talked to me about the power of changing my story—of seeing the blessing in the curse—that I could use what happened to my to help others. He saw my potential and encouraged me.

I finished my Associate's degree with a 3.8 grade point average. Then, I completed my Bachelor's degree with a 3.9 and my Master's degree with a 4.0, and received all A's in my coursework for a Ph.D. in psychology.

I went from failing to earning straight A's. Was it because I became smarter? No. It was because my perception, my story, of myself changed.

When I graduated with my Master's degree, I opened a youth counseling center in honor of my brother. And, while my life took me down a different path shortly after I opened the center, it fulfilled my dream and opened a new door.

When I posted an ad looking for someone to take over my business, it was Natalie who answered the ad. It wasn't until a couple years later that we came together, both as life and business partners, but the closing of one chapter was clearly the beginning of another.

This brings me to my final story of transformation—changing my beliefs and patterns in relationships.

Rethinking Relationships

Throughout my childhood, the relationships I experienced and observed in my life were filled with chaos and conflict. To me, it was normal. As most people do, I mirrored those same patterns in my personal relationships as an adult. After many years of pain and finding myself in the same relationship over and over again, and after years of studying psychology and realizing my life experience was because of my conditioning, I decided it was time to change. I recognized the continuation of my story from childhood and decided to tell a new story for my future.

I created what I call a "non-negotiable list", which outlined all of the characteristics I wanted in a happy, healthy romantic relationship and all of the traits wanted in my ideal partner. My list also included the characteristics and traits that I would no longer accept and tolerate in my life. I made sure to include only the items that were truly non-negotiable, meaning I knew in my heart I would not ever be okay with these characteristics or traits. With this new list, I wrote all of my old patterns and dramas and pains from past relationships out of my new story.

It was shortly after this decision to change that I met Natalie, and she met all of my "non-negotiables". Not surprisingly, she had her own "list" too—it turns out we were a perfect match. And the rest was history.

3: THE 6 HUMAN NEEDS

At the core, our decisions and behaviors are driven by underlying needs and our beliefs about how these needs must be met. The 6 human needs are a powerful psychological framework, created by therapist Cloé Madanes and popularized by Anthony Robbins' strategic intervention strategies. These core needs are at the root of our motivations and why we prioritize certain decisions and actions, often without our awareness. Each person values one or more of these needs more than the others. Which need is your primary driver is a huge determining factor for how you live your life.

The 6 human needs are:

1. Certainty/comfort
2. Uncertainty/variety
3. Significance
4. Love and connection
5. Growth
6. Contribution

The first four needs are called the needs of the personality. These four needs are things that we always find ways to meet them—they are vital. The last two are called the needs of the spirit and are needs not always met. In most cases, the first four needs must be met before a person is able to start to value and focus on meeting the last 2 needs. However, when we meet those higher-level needs is when we truly feel fulfilled. Now let's look at each of them.

Need 1: Certainty/Comfort

At our core we want to feel that we are in control of our reality. This feeling gives us security. This allows us to feel comfortable in our life to feel that we can avoid pain and create pleasure. At the core this is just a survival mechanism that we have. Certainty makes us feel safe, emotionally, psychologically, and physically. Depending on how much we value certainty will depend how much risk we take in life. You probably have met people on both ends of the spectrum—those who want to control every single detail in their life and those that crave uncertainty. The extreme need for certainty, however, will hold you back because all growth and change requires uncertainty.

Need 2: Uncertainty/Variety

The second one is uncertainty. Yes, it's the opposite of the first one. Think about it—what would happen if you always knew everything that would happen to you? You would probably be bored to death. So, uncertainty brings excitement and spice to life. The level of uncertainty that you are willing and able to live with determines how much and how fast you will change. Keep in mind that being able to deal with uncertainty is also a skill that can be developed, as you become more confident that you can deal with change. Also, as you start associating uncertainty and change with something that create happiness and helps you achieve your dreams, your desire for certainty will increase.

Need 3: Significance

Think about it, we all want to feel like we are special. We want to feel like we are important, needed and unique. There are a variety of ways that we can get significance. For example, you can get it by feeling like you are the best at something, by making a lot of money, having the best house in your neighborhood, by buying the latest thing, getting a master's degree or a doctorate, by becoming a social influencer, by being the best dad, having a bunch of tattoos, you can even be that person that has more problems that anyone else, the most intimidating, or even the most spiritual person. As you can see that there are endless ways to feel significant. People will go to great lengths to feel significant in their life.

Need 4: Love & Connection

The next need is Love and Connection. Whether we realize it or not, love is that thing that we need more than anything. When we love 100% we feel alive and it is a powerful force. For love, many people are willing to do extortionary things for others, whether it's the love that a parent has for a child or the love of a romantic relationship. However, if we don't feel like we can get love, we settle for connection—even if these connections do not serve us. There are a lot of ways to get connection, whether it is through a friendship, a pet or even connecting to nature. Less-constructive ways of getting connection are through social media, sacrificing our authenticity to conform to a group, or people pleasing.

Need 5: Growth

The next one is the need for growth. Think about it if you're not growing in an area of your life, then that area is dying. This can be your relationship, your business, or an aspect of your personal life. If you are not growing than it does not matter what you are creating in your exterior world. That need for certainty can hold you back from growth, leading you to feel empty and not be able to feel true fulfillment. Growth can be scary because it can have uncertainty for some, but it brings fulfillment.

Need 6: Contribution

The last one is contribution and its one that many people reflect on in the later stages of life, as we look at our legacy. Contribution is like a higher level of the need for significance, the difference being that it's no longer about you. However, contribution is the essence of life. Life is not about me… it's about us. We are social creatures and we have a natural need to feel that we have a higher purpose and that our life has meaning. The way we find that is to contribution to others. In fact, the feeling that we are contributing to others can helps us overcome the biggest changes if we think it has a purpose. Life therefore is about creating meaning, and that comes from giving.

So, which need a person values most, and which ones they are starving to meet, will influence the choices that they make in life. They will find a way to meet those needs one way or another, whether through a negative or positive way. For example, someone robbing someone can feel significant, have that thrill of uncertainty, and at the same time they feel certain because they are the one in control. So, this negative action can meet 3 core needs.

The power of identifying your own hierarchy of needs (which one/s are most important to you) is that you can then reflect to see if you're meeting your needs in constructive ways. (And, if not, consciously choose more constructive ways of meeting your needs.)

At the end of the day, fulfillment comes from something internal—whether, deep inside you feel loved, feel like you are growing, and contributing to others. This is why the higher level needs (further down the list) are what ultimately lead to fulfillment. However, in most cases, the lower level needs HAVE to be met in order for a person to turn their attention to the higher level needs.

Let's look at constructive ways of meeting these needs:

- **Certainty**: You can have certainty by having a daily routine or having a community around you that is supportive no matter what's happening in your life.

- **Variety**: You can have variety by adding diverse experiences to your life. You can also try new things and learn new skills.

- **Significance**: You can meet the need of significance by using your talents and skills. You can also master a skill and share your skills with others.

- **Love/Connection**: You can meet this need by establishing life-long friendships spending more time with likeminded people, as well as improving your relationship skills.

- **Growth**: You can meet the need for growth by constantly learning. For example, reading new books, watching YouTube videos, or following others that help you grow. You can also surround yourself with people that motivate you and challenge you to become a better person.

- **Contribution**: You can meet the need of contribution by sharing your talents and passions with others. You can also engage in causes that are meaningful to you.

So, ask yourself

- Which needs are the most important to you?

- How do you currently meet these needs?

- Which area of need are you currently struggling with the most?

- In what way do you feel like your need is not being met?

- What do you believe is necessary for your need to be met?

- How can you meet these needs in a way that will help you truly be fulfilled?

4: IT'S BREAKTHROUGH TIME! BREAKING THE CHANGE CYCLE

Nothing in life stands still. Science has shown us that the entire human body—every cell—completely regenerates itself within a span of about seven years. Brain scientists and psychologists have agreed that in each moment our brains are taking in new information and our minds are constantly assimilating this information into our neural network of thoughts, beliefs, and associations.

You cannot have a new experience without it literally changing your mind, and life cannot exist without continuous growth and expansion. You are actually changing as you read these words. You are moving, growing, expanding, and changing. It is no secret that the world around you is constantly changing as well.

We live in a time of unprecedented change, as technology expands our reach and capabilities and as global connectivity transforms our borders and cultures.

There is no question: You are changing. The wonderful thing is that you have the power and ability to direct changes in your life. In fact, what you feel, think, say, and believe about your life is constantly putting change into motion, regardless of whether you realize it or not.

You are creating your life as you go along, so you might as well create it intentionally.

All that is required is a choice. YOU ARE AT A CHOICE POINT. You can choose to continue on with your life as you currently are living it, letting the external world and your past dictate what you experience, or you can choose to create your life to be everything that you dream.

Understanding the Change Cycle

Even if your gung-ho about transforming your life, there is an important obstacle you need to address in order to be successful. Most people find deliberate change to be a difficult process. Many well-intentioned people have changes they want to make in their lives, but they get stuck repeating the same "change cycle" over and over again. Below you'll find this common cycle, and you'll most likely find it to sound oddly familiar because most people experience this process of inspiration and resistance when they face a decision to change.

1. **Discontent:** You grow increasingly unhappy and discontent with an area of your life. You "hang in there," tolerate, ignore, repress, or otherwise deal with the circumstance because it is comfortable and familiar, and you fear change.

2. **Breaking Point**: Eventually your level of discontent builds high enough that you cannot take it anymore. You reach a "breaking point," either through exhaustion or due to a dramatic event occurring that triggers the break.

3. **Decision**: You decide you're ready to change and declare that you will no longer tolerate the undesirable situation. You take the first step toward change, giving you a short-lived sense of hope.

4. **Fear**: Usually, shortly (or immediately) after your feelings of empowerment, you encounter your fear. You become uncomfortable and anxious about the idea of changing. You doubt your decision. Both options look bleak. You feel helpless, empty.

5. **Amnesia**: The fear of change grows strong enough that it makes the original situation look much better than you originally thought. You perceive the original situation as less anxiety-producing than the change. You're used to it; it's comfortable; it's familiar. Plus, it has become part of your identity, so you resist letting it go. You temporarily forget why you wanted to change it so badly.

6. **Backtracking**: Most people choose to go back to or stick with the item they wished to change. You essentially talk yourself out of changing.

Inevitably, you soon will find yourself unhappy and discontent once again. Your level of pain will continue to increase until you reach another breaking point, this time even more extreme and more painful. This cycle will continue until one of two things happen:

1. **Extreme Pain:** You have a breaking point that is severe enough to push through the change cycle. For many people, unfortunately, it takes an extreme circumstance to push them to evolve, such as major financial loss, job loss, loss of a loved one, the ending of a relationship, a severe accident, or a nervous breakdown. You see, your Higher Self knows what you truly want and will lead you to it. If you resist changing long enough, something will happen in your life that will put you in a position where you have NO CHOICE but to change.

   You do not need to wait until there's a flood to move your home away from the shoreline.

2. **Self-Honesty:** You have the humbling experience of realizing that

there's a part of you that doesn't really want to change. You are comfortable with your habits, with what you know. You have a lot of fear that holds you back. You have many self-limiting beliefs. You receive some sort of benefit from staying where you are. You are unhappy because you want to be unhappy. You are addicted to the situation. You believe your pain is you; it's your story. You can see your resistance to letting it go. Only after reaching this level of self-honesty can you truly choose to change.

Can you see how this change cycle has impacted your life? Are you ready for it to stop? Have you experienced change amnesia before? If so, you know that the more you move toward the changes you want the stronger your fear and resistance will become. Are you ready to swallow the pill of self-honesty, even if it is hard, because you are tired of being dissatisfied? Are you ready to take responsibility for your life and create the life you dream of having? Are you at the point where you will accept nothing less than what you truly want?

Consider the following reasons you may have been allowing yourself to fall victim to this cycle:

You don't want to change. You don't really want the thing you think you want. You may be trying to convince yourself to change to appease others or conform to what you believe you "should" do. If you don't want to change, accept it. This is very common with people who say they want to quit smoking. They don't really WANT to quit, they simply think they SHOULD quit. It never works. You have to want it.

You don't know what you want. You don't know what you really want or you're not allowing yourself to think about what you really want because you don't think you can have it. So, you end up thinking you want things that aren't what you TRULY want, and your Higher Self knows it. You'll never feel inspired enough to follow through on change if it isn't even what you want. Try imagining what you would want if time, money, and people did not limit you.

Your dream isn't big enough. The reward isn't big enough. You aren't excited. Happiness is excitement. Passion is what makes you willing to endure to attain a goal. What would you do ANYTHING to attain?

You're letting your fear be bigger than you. You don't believe you can do it. You don't trust yourself. You put everyone else before yourself. You'd rather tolerate severe pain than face temporary discomfort. Are you really willing to settle? Isn't the fear of being stuck in a life you don't want and missing out on your dreams more painful than the temporary experience of changing?

You are attached to your problem. Your ego and identity are wrapped up in your problem, and you fear that if you let go of your problem you'll have nothing to talk about. Who would you be? Would it be better?

You're benefiting from your problem. The benefit you're receiving from NOT changing is bigger than your perceived benefit from changing. It gives you an excuse and something to talk about. It allows you to hide deeper issues from yourself and others. What are you holding onto? How does it benefit you to NOT change?

Failure no longer has to be an option. Neither does doing nothing and staying stuck where you are. If you're facing a potential change that's nagging at you to be made, take some time in self-reflection and be brutally honest with yourself. Is your desire for more, for fulfillment, for happiness finally strong enough that you are willing to encounter the obstacles and endure the fear? If so, congratulations, you will succeed—you are ready to break through!

Self-Honesty Reflection

- Can you see how this change cycle has impacted your life?

- Are you ready for it to stop?

- Have you experienced change amnesia before?

- What will happen if you continue NOT to change?

- Are you ready to swallow the pill of self-honesty, even if it is hard, because you are tired of being dissatisfied?

- Are you ready to take responsibility for your life and create the life you dream of having?

- Are you at the point where you will accept nothing less than what you truly want?

SECTION 3: YOUR HERO'S JOURNEY

1: GIVING YOUR PAIN A PURPOSE

We all have pain. It's inevitable. It's part of life. But, the first thing we want to get clear is that there's a difference between pain and suffering. Pain happens when your life circumstances do not match up with your view of the way the world should be. Suffering is when you feel powerless over it. You are never powerless over it. You can always change your point of view.

Why do bad things happen?

Many people resist the notion that we can change our view of the world in order to stop ourselves from suffering. Sometimes bad things happen and they are so unacceptable that we don't want to find a better way of feeling about them. We feel resentful. We feel angry. We feel wronged. Depending upon our belief system or "view of the world" we deal with our "curses" in different ways. Below are several common belief systems about why bad things happen:

- Everything in life is predestined, as part of a greater Cosmic Plan.
- An outside force (God, the Universe, Source, etc) is directing our lives and causes bad things to happen to teach us lessons.
- Everything happens by random chance and comes down to bad or good luck.
- Before we were born we pre-planned the events of our lives to learn certain lessons.
- We create our lives through our intentions, emotions, and actions (Law of Attraction).
- Everything is someone else's fault.

As you can imagine, whether we experience pain and/or suffering is largely due to which belief system we choose. If you would like to choose not to suffer any longer, consider the following tools:

Scratching the Scab

Some people are acutely aware of their pain. In fact, many people are so focused on their pain that they forget to enjoy life. Our culture teaches us to find our connection to others by commiserating about our pain. But most of the time our true pain gets locked tightly beneath the surface.

Our culture may push pain as a social connection technique, but it also does a good hard sell of repression as a preferred coping tactic. Most people have become comfortable with hiding from their pain. They cannot be their authentic selves because in order to know how they really feel, what they really want, and who they really are they would have to be whole. You can't be whole if you are cutting off parts of yourself.

By hiding our pain we stifle our greatness.

If this is resonating with you and you feel that there is repressed pain beneath the surface, we challenge you to scratch the scab. Stop holding yourself back by denying yourself. (Please seek support by those who are qualified to help you.)

Drop the Water Line

People are like icebergs; we see only 10 percent.

Most of the time we only see people's identity, roles, and the pain they select as their social connection tool. The 90 percent below the surface contains who they really are: their biggest fears and deepest longings; what sustains them and what breaks them down, their talents, creativity, and brilliance, as well as their faults, failings, and mistakes.

My call to action is to challenge yourself to show more of what is beneath the surface—the good and the bad. When you are open and honest about your pain you will be surprised how many other people you meet have either experienced what you have or can otherwise relate to your pain.

Knowing that you are not alone is a huge force for healing. One of the most powerful healing experiences you can give another person is to be the witness for their pain.

Giving Your Pain a Purpose

Now, whether your default coping strategy is to repress your pain or dwell in it, in either case you can heal by giving your pain a purpose.

Ask yourself the following questions:

- Did you learn anything from that which caused your pain?

- Has your pain inspired you to do something you otherwise would not have?

- Has the result of the situation pushed you to make a change that bettered your life?

- Is there something meaningful you could do to help others going through the same thing?

Successful, happy people have one thing in common—they turn their curses into blessings.

As Albert Einstein points out, you have a choice:

> *"There are two ways to live: you can live as if nothing is a miracle; you can live as if everything is a miracle."*

2: INTRODUCING THE HERO'S JOURNEY

If you've ever watched a move or read a story, you know that at the center of every story is a hero. This hero isn't usually a superhero who is endowed with super-human powers. In most cases, the hero is an ordinary person who either has to rise to the occasion when life throws them a catastrophe or who has to face their demons in order to create a better life. If you think about it, even the Superheroes usually start out as a regular guy or gal. Think the nerdy Clark Kent who becomes Superman or the timid Frodo Baggins who saves the world in the Lord of the Rings.

Not only do most stories follow the tale of a hero's journey, but that journey tends to follow a similar path. In fact, this same journey narrative has been used over and over again since as long as humans have been telling stories. Joseph Campbell is famous for his work dedicated to exploring why the specific steps in the hero's journey are so consistent throughout the history of storytelling, as well as the psychology behind why humans are so intrigued with stories.

The 12-steps of the hero's journey, as solidified by Campbell, are used in movies and literature because it works. The human mind finds a story that follows this process irresistible. We simply cannot turn away from our hero— we want to know what happens to them—we want them to succeed. Stories and mythologies help point to beyond that which humans can understand with rational thought... they point to the source and meaning of life.

Whether the hero embarks on an intentional quest or is propelled into an unintentional journey, it becomes a serendipitous adventure. The stories may be about the slaying of dragons or overcoming overwhelming odds, but the truth is that all hero myths are about transformation of consciousness. The death of the old person and the birth of another (the hero).

The greatest act of courage is taking the journey into yourself. The moral objective of every tale is pushing beyond perceived limits and sacrificing or dedicating oneself to a cause greater than one's self.

These stories draw us in because we can relate to them. Each of us sees a little part of ourselves in every unsuspecting hero. We relate to their feelings of dissatisfaction, their dream for a better life, the fear they face stepping into the unknown, the frustrations of their struggles, and the glory of victory. We live out the dream we hold in our hearts through the stories we watch on the big screen. When an ordinary person does extraordinary things, it gives us hope. It tells us that maybe, just maybe, we can do it too.

And the truth is, we are each the hero in our own life's journey. We relate to the 12 steps of the hero's journey because it IS our journey. The reason humans have connected to this storyline for thousands of years is that it is the human storyline. The hero's journey is our destiny!

And so, let's explore the traditional hero's journey, what each step looks like, and how your own life experience fits into it. The beautiful thing about exploring your own hero's journey is that you get to become the playwright. You get to write the script. As you go through the activity, write down what experiences you have had in your life that unfolded like that part of the journey. Try to identify where along the journey you are now, and where you've been. You find that you have already completed the hero's journey, maybe even more than once! Or perhaps you're at a pivotal moment when you're answering the call, seeking a mentor, or facing a great challenge.

By looking at your own life, and your current situation, through the lens of the hero's journey, you can see yourself more objectively. You may be able to see what is happening more clearly, including where the story is leading. In the end, the hero always transforms and returns back to the life they knew before a changed person—a better person—better able to make the difference they are meant to make in the world.

3: YOUR HERO'S JOURNEY ACTIVITY

Now that you can see how powerful storytelling is for the transformation of the human mind and spirit, it's time to look at the 12 steps of the hero's journey and how it relates to your own life. There are no right or wrong answers here. Simply reflect on each step and check in with yourself to see what experiences from your own life you can relate to that stage of the journey. You may have experienced more than one journey in your lifetime. Every time there is a calling—a problem that pulls you to face a challenge or change—the hero (you) is being beckoned to a new adventure.

So, you can go through this activity imagining it starting early in your life and addressing the first big challenge you faced, or you can address the most recent challenge—the one you might be experiencing right now. And in the end, your answers to the questions about your experiences within each stage may not fit together chronologically. The story might not unfold like a movie. In fact, it probably won't. But that's not the point. The point is that by looking at your life this way, you will be able to see that you, too, are on the path of a hero. You, too, will transform and fulfill your destiny. Trust the journey. (For this writing activity, you will need additional paper.)

Step 1: Ordinary Life

Most of the time, the hero starts out living a normal, every-day life. Everything is familiar, comfortable. They feel uneasy, uncomfortable, dissatisfied. Then, something happens that wakes them up to the fact that something is wrong.

In your life, what were the first stirrings of dissatisfaction or unease? What happened to wake you up to the need for change?

[handwritten: maring, turning 50, feeling this nudge to help others, use my strengths.]

Step 2: The Call

[handwritten: w/ advertising]

Depending on the hero, the problem could be external—such as a catastrophe happening in the world around them. For others, the problem is internal, such as becoming aware of a deep dissatisfaction with some aspect of life. After being exposed to this information, the hero feels called to do something about it. The hero is challenged to take action and step into the unknown.

In your life, what are you feeling called to do? Remember, this could be a calling that already happened or that is happening now. (This could be many different things: advance your career, pursue a passion, improve your health, change a relationship, start a business, support a cause, etc.)

[handwritten: Evaluated my strengths, feel an internal calling to coach, guide, support]

Step 3: Refusal of the Call

Often, at first the hero fails to answer the call. They are afraid of what it will take. They don't think they can do it. They think it will be to hard. They feel insecure, inadequate. Their familiar life of comfort calls them to resist this new adventure. They hesitate. But, they become increasingly aware that there are real consequences if they do not act. Something meaningful will be lost.

In your life, what fears or resistance did you experience after becoming aware of the problem that is/was calling you to action? What additional situations or information were you presented with that further helped you see what was at stake? What are/were you going to lose?

[handwritten: ① unsure of exactly what? how ② fear/insecurity held me back, thinking I wasn't like others instead of how I related to others]

Step 4: The Guide

In most stories, the hero meets a guide, a mentor, or a helper that provides vital advice and points them in the right direction. The timing of the appearance of the guide varies, and so if the hero refuses the call, often a helper of some type appears to nudge them into answering the call. Sometimes the guide continues to return to the hero to help them move along their journey, however the guide never "saves" the hero or do anything for them. The hero does not need to be saved. But, at the same time, the hero never does it all alone.

In your life, who have been your guides? You can list all people who have influenced you, including mentors who do not know that you see them as a guide, such as authors of books you read. However, make sure to identify what guidance you have received that SPECIFICALLY relates to this story. Throughout the rest of the steps in the journey, make a note any time a guide (the same guide or new ones) provides additional advice or direction. Guides: Molly, uncaged, my friends,

CLIENTS: Anne & Barb

Step 5: The Threshold

This is the pivotal moment when the hero officially leaves the ordinary world and steps into the journey in a way that they cannot turn back. This is the decision point. This is when the hero begins their quest!

In your life, what decision point have you experienced? (Are you there now?) What IS the threshold—the pivotal moment? Imagine you stepped from your old life into your new life—what would be that actual step? (This could be an internal decision, a public commitment, a phone call, physically going some place, making a purchase, enrolling in something, something symbolic, etc.) Also, what exactly IS your quest, your journey? What would you call it? Give it a name.

Step 6: The Road of Trails

The entire purpose of a quest is for the hero to learn, grow, and, well, become the hero. In order for this to happen, there are inevitably obstacles to overcome, challenges to meet, and tests of strength of will. The hero will learn the rules of this new world. There will be moments of victory and moments of defeat. The hero will meet allies who help them face their foes. This is the action and adventure part of the story that keeps people engaged, wanting to know more. If the hero just went right from the decision to the victory, no one would watch. And it wouldn't make for a very fulfilling real-life story either. There is always more meaning in the underdog story, right?

In your life, what obstacles or challenges have you faced (or are you facing)? How has your strength of commitment and will been tested? What are the rules of this new world? How are they different from your old life? What victories have you had? In what ways have you failed? Who are your allies? Your enemies?

Step 7: The Approach of the Innermost Cave

This is the turning point, when the hero finally goes all-in. They reach the point when they are 100% certain what must be done. They are ready to accept the risks and the possibility of failure. This second decision point happens when the hero approaches the innermost cave. This next threshold can be something literal, such as having to enter the cave which contains what the hero fears most or the ultimate challenge the hero must face. It can also be entering into the hero's darkest places, their inner conflict, their demons. The hero prepares to face the one, big thing that they have been putting off. Often the hero rests briefly to reflect on the journey, summons the courage to face the treacherous road that awaits. Tension escalates in anticipation of the ultimate test.

In your life, what is the innermost cave? What is the one, big challenge? What decision must you make? If you find yourself at this point now, this is the perfect time to be reflecting on your journey, which gives you the courage to see how far you've come and that your life has been preparing you for this moment. You are ready. How are you feeling? If you were the guide, what would you tell the hero at this moment?

Step 8: The Ordeal

This is the ultimate test. In movies, this part is called the climax—it's the peak of the action. The hero must face their greatest fear or face their most terrifying foe. One way or another, the hero must face death, whether literal or figurative. The hero uses the skills and experiences they picked up along their journey through the challenges and their innermost cave in order to face this final challenge. It's the hero's moment of truth. Everything is put on the line and the hero moves forward knowing nothing will ever be the same. It can't, this must be done. And looking back, it is obvious that this moment was inevitable.

In your life, what is the "death" you will face? (The fear, the situation, or the foe.) What skills and experiences have you picked up along your journey that will serve you now? What, exactly, must you do? Can you see that your entire life has been leading up to this moment?

Step 9: The Transformation and Reward

The hero defeated the enemy, survived, overcame. But more than anything, the hero transformed, like a butterfly emerging from its cocoon. Out of the ashes of death rises a phoenix of symbolic rebirth. The hero receives a reward in some from, whether it is recognition, power, wisdom, reconciliation, a treasure, but in the end, no matter the price, the true reward is always the glory of personal transformation itself. The real change is internal.

In your life, what will this transformation look like? How will you feel? What will be different? How will you be different? What reward will

35

you enjoy? Why will it all have been worth it?

Step 10: The Road Back

The hero cannot relax and enjoy the thrill of victory for long. The hero feels another call—to return home—to share the spoils of the reward or bring what was learned to those they care about. The journey is not over. With reward in hand and transformation in heart, the hero charts the path back. But the road can be filled with additional risks and dangers. A villain may appear who seeks to steal the reward. Unresolved issues must be dealt with. The hero may face their shadow. These additional roadblocks challenge the hero to internalize what they've learned and prove to themselves that they have, in fact, changed for good. It is in this stage of the journey that the quest is won, or lost.

In your life, what does "returning home" represent? How are you going to use what you have learned or accomplished? Who will you help or what will you do with it? At this point, what unresolved issues do you anticipate having to face? What other obstacles do you anticipate will pop-up in response to your transformation? What shadows may be lurking?

Step 11: Rebirth

This is the moment the hero crosses the final threshold—the final test of the hero's true growth. The hero is tested for the final time—it is their moment to demonstrate their mastery and step into their power. This battle pushes the hero to defeat their limitations and release their old self, once and for all. They return home a hero.

In your life, after transforming, defeating your foes or reaching your goals, what final battle may you need to face? Is there another step in this journey that you need to take in order to fully be able to feel as though you are "home" and able to integrate everything you've learned in your life? What would it take to embrace your new self, 100%?

Step 12: Return with the Elixir

When the hero returns to his ordinary world, a changed person, they will have something to share with those back home. This could be a solution to a problem, a new perspective of life, a resource, or some sort of resolution with key players. Sometimes the hero faces doubters or is even punished for the journey. But, in the end, the hero always shares what they've learned or acquired with those who they did it all for. That is, after all, what makes them a hero.

In your life, what is the elixir you are bringing back with you from your journey? Who are you going to share it with? How are you going to pay forward what you learned? What difference are you going to make in the world? Will there be any haters or doubters? If so, how can you remind yourself that you didn't do it for them, you did it because it was your destiny to be the hero of your own life.

Regardless of where you find yourself along your personal adventure, the hero's journey shows you that you are always exactly where you are supposed to be. All you need to do is take the next step.

And as your journey continues to unfold, remember that it's not about avoiding problems, it's about what you learn while overcoming th~ not about perfection, it's about progress. It's not about b or popular, it's about becoming YOU. And it's not just about how you use your life experience to make a greater

Journey on.

Notes

SECTION 4: WHAT DO YOU REALLY WANT?

1: IDENTIFYING WHAT YOU REALLY WANT

So, what do you want? If you're like most people, this is surprisingly difficult to answer. Most people are so inundated with messages from their parents, peers, and society of what they "should" want that their true desires are drowned out. Plus, even if they've held dreams and desires in the past, their life experiences have lead them to believe that what they want is not possible, and so they stop allowing themselves to want it. They tell themselves "I can't have that" and it hurts to want something they cannot have, and so they stop thinking about it. They give it up. They settle.

But, the good news is that dreams can never die—deep down you know what you want. It tugs at you from within, but you may be so used to ignoring it that you no longer notice.

Forgotten Dreams

What do you REALLY want? Answer this without allowing other people's opinions or beliefs limit you. Answer this without thinking about limitations—imagine for a moment that money is not an issue and that whatever that is currently blocking you is magically taken care of.

What are things you wanted, desired or dreamed about that at some point you decided you could NOT have and so stopped wanting them? This could have been in childhood or adulthood. You may not have allowed yourself to think about these desires in a long time. For each one, ask yourself if this is something that you STILL want. If not, cross it out and let it go. Circle any desires that you feel a strong emotional reaction to when you think about them.

Identifying What You Do NOT Want

For many people it's easier to identify what they do NOT want than what they DO want. When asked what they want, many people respond "not this!" So, to start, simply make a list of the things you know for sure you do NOT want in your life. These can be things that USED to be in your life that you never want to experience again. They can be things CURRENTLY in your life that you would like to stop. They can be things you are simply certain you never want in your FUTURE.

Once you know what you do NOT want, it will help you identify what you DO want. Ask yourself, "What is the opposite of what I don't want?" or "If I know I do NOT want ____, then it means that I do want ____."

I do NOT want...	The opposite (what I DO want)

Getting More Specific

You have determined some things you want and don't want. You have determined the roles, beliefs and ego states that have influenced your life story and the new perspectives you can now take of them. Now, it is time to delve into greater detail about what you WANT your life to be. You can always add to this activity later, as you learn more about your desires.

Once you begin asking yourself about what you want, you'll find yourself noticing more and more things that make you think, "yes, I want this!" It's okay if you're still not sure what you want. Allow your desire to grow over time. Throughout your day, simply notice whether you like or dislike certain things, people, situations or experiences.

Say, "Yes, I want more of this!" to the things you like.

Say, "No, thank you." to the things you do not like. Saying "thank you" acknowledges that you appreciate the ability to identify what you don't want because it helps you know more clearly what you DO want.

Digging Deeper into "Why"

Only if you have a big enough reason will you be committed to creating lasting change. And, the only way your reason to change your life will be big enough is if you understand your core reasons. Below is an example that will help illustrate the point.

A student in one of our classes once told us, "I can't wait to go home and start using these efficiency techniques to make my work more effective and productive" And so we asked, "Well, why do you want to be more productive?" The student said that it would help her to get a promotion at work. We asked her why she would want a promotion and she said "So I can get a raise." So we asked again, "Why do you want a raise" and she said "Because I need the money to buy a larger home". So we asked "Why?" and she says because I want my mother and sister to move in with me". "Why?" "Because it has been our dream to own a big house together and live together as a family."

To which we responded, "Good, NOW you have identified what you really want. It's a large house with your family living with you. You don't really want to be more efficient. What you want is the experience of having your family living with you."

Look at the dreams and desires you identified above. For each, ask yourself the following questions:

- Why does this matter to you?

- Why?

- How would it make you feel?

- What would happen if I didn't have, do, or be this?

- Why does that matter?

- Why?

Keep probing and asking yourself until you get to the core of the issue. In some cases, you will find that your deeper motive is a specific desire, like in the example above. However, often the core motivation beneath your desire is actually an emotional state that you wish to experience. In fact, everything we want is because we believe it will make us feel the way we desire: good, or at least better.

Get Other People Out of Your Head

Lastly, consider if any of the things you "want" are truly only because you think you "should" want them. It's easy to unknowingly adopt other people's dreams. Get other people's voices and beliefs out of your head... then take a final look at your desires and confirm that this is TRULY what you want.

2: THE WHEEL OF LIFE: IDENTIFYING WHAT AREAS NEED YOUR ATTENTION

The Wheel is a simple but powerful tool designed to help you get a graphical representation of the present balance between different areas regarding your life and business which will most benefit you by improving.

The eight sections in the Wheel of Life (on the next page) represent different aspects of your life. Seeing the center of the wheel as 1 and the outer edges as 10, rank your level of satisfaction with each life area by filling in that piece of the pie to that level.

You can use the 8 categories in this sample or determine the 6 to 12 most important categories in your life and business to create your own wheel. Use the following questions to help you determine how you would rate each life area on a scale of 1 to 10.

Career (Business)	Money
Is my business rewarding? Does it reflect my values? Do I feel balanced, in control, and happy with my time, responsibilities, etc?	Do I earn enough through my business? Am I happy with how I spend it? Am I on a path to financial freedom?
Health	**Significant other/ Romance**
Am I generally fit and well? Do I eat healthily? Do I exercise regularly?	Do I have/want a good relationship? Do we share values and intimacy? Am I nurturing the relationship and giving it the attention it needs?
Friends and Family	**Personal Growth**
Do I have/want a close circle of friends? Do I spend enough time with family and friends? Do I value the relationship we have with each other?	Am I continually learning new things? Do I enjoy new opportunities for growth? Are the things I do growing me as a person?
Fun and Recreation	**Physical Environment**
Do I have fun often? Do I know how to relax? Do I enjoy sports or have hobbies or take time for myself?	Do I like the area in which I live? Is my home comfortable, tidy and warm? Is my office conducive to productivity?

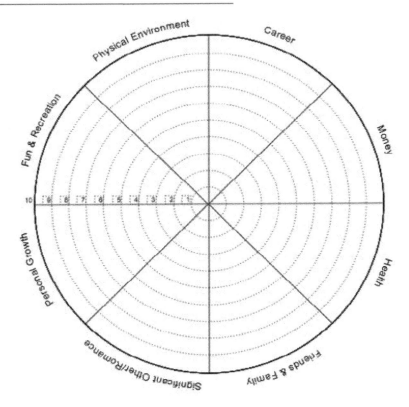

Interpreting Your Wheel

If this were a real wheel, how bumpy would the ride be? In theory, what you are aiming for with your completed wheel is to have all segments scored evenly (or close), above 7 and as near 10 as possible. Because not all areas are EQUAL in priority to you, consider marking each with a priority ranking of 1 (low) to 10 (high). Also, when determining how you rank each segment, rank each by asking "how balanced and satisfied am I with this one area" rather than comparing it to others.

Remember, balanced does NOT mean EQUAL.

If you have any particularly low scores you will want to make those areas of your life a priority. However, it's not always cut and dry. It is necessary to investigate how they may interact with each other in order to identify the area to address first.

For example, Fun & Recreation scored low could be tied to a low score regarding Money. Not having sufficient money could mean that a person may be unable to go out or engage in recreation that has an appreciable cost associated with it, which can lead to a low level of morale and lack of desire to have fun. A low score for Money could also be tied to the low score for Career/Business, though it may be that money is low due to poor financial management. Also, a low score for Fun & Recreation may be linked to Career/Business if time requirements and time management have cause in imbalance.

The purpose here is to determine if a low score in one category is the result of other factors. Improvement in one area will have an impact on other areas as well. At the same time, making changes in one area may have temporary or long term impact on other areas. For example, if some- one makes changes in their business, such as to increase productivity and eliminate unnecessary busy work, they may have more free time, and as a result their Fun & Recreation, Romance, or Friends & Family categories may increase as well.

Questions to Determine Goals

Use the following questions to dig deeper and uncover your desired outcomes and what you can do to improve your balance.

- Have you ever been higher than the number you have recorded?

- What was actually happening when you were higher up the scale?

- Have you ever been lower than the number you have recorded?

- What did you do to move up the scale?

- What have you learnt from previously being lower on the scale?

- What number on the scale do you want to be?

- What exactly do you want?

- What actions can you take to start moving up the scale?

- What will you be like when you have achieved this?

- What will be the impact of achieving this on other areas of your life?

- How will achieving this affect others close to you?

- What will achieving this bring you that you want?

- What will achieving this bring you that you don't want?

- What skills do you already have that will assist you in achieving this?

- What skills do you want to gain that will assist you in achieving this?

- Where can you learn these skills?

- What other options do you have?

- What would need to happen for you to move up one point on the scale by this time next week?

Use the answers to these questions to develop your plan and action steps.

SECTION 5: WHO DO YOU REALLY WANT TO BE?

1: IDENTITY CHECK-IN: WHO YOU TRULY ARE VS. WHO YOU ARE BEING

If you imagine your life like a play, you would see that you play a character in this play. This character is a ROLE that you are playing. In fact, the character has multiple roles that it plays.

Make a list of the roles you play in life. There are generally 2 categories: career and relationships. You most likely play multiple roles in the "relationships" category, such as parent, spouse, child, etc. You may play more than one role under the "career" category too, such as "programmer" and "manager".

Then, complete these questions for each IMPORTANT role.

Career

- What is your career? (Fireman, teacher, sales, programmer, etc)

- What role do you play in that career? (employee, manager, entrepreneur, support-role, problem-solver, etc)

- What are the traits, behaviors, and qualities of a person who is playing this role "correctly"?

- What are the traits, behaviors, and qualities of a person who is playing this role "incorrectly"?

- How does how YOU act out this role compare to what you believe you "should" be doing?

- Where did you learn how to play this role? Who taught or demonstrated this?

- Do you truly believe that the definition you have identified for this role is "correct"? If not, how would you change it?

- Does it feel right for you to be playing this role the way you are playing it now? Does it feel right to be playing this role AT ALL?

- How would you need to play the role differently in order for it to be in integrity with your true self?

Relationships

- What roles do you play in your relationships? (For example: father, mother, child, brother, sister, grandparent, boyfriend, girlfriend, wife, husband, friend, neighbor, etc) (YOU WILL WANT TO COMPLETE THE QUESTIONS BELOW FOR EACH OF RELATIONSHIP ROLES YOU IDENTIFY. USE THE NOTES SPACE PROVIDED OR ADDITIONAL PAPER.)

- What are the traits, behaviors, and qualities of a person who is playing this role "correctly"?

- What are the traits, behaviors, and qualities of a person who is playing this role "incorrectly"?

- How does how YOU act out this role compare to what you believe you "should" be doing?

- Where did you learn how to play this role? Who taught or demonstrated this?

- Do you truly believe that the definition you have identified for this role is "correct"? If not, how would you change it?

- Does it feel right for you to be playing this role the way you are playing it now? Does it feel right to be playing this role AT ALL?

- How would you need to play the role differently in order for it to be in integrity with your true self?

Notes:

Final Questions

- Who, if anyone, would be affected by you letting go of (or change) the roles that don't serve you?

- What benefit do you get from maintain these roles the way they are?

- What benefits would you get from removing or changing them?

- Who you would be if the roles you don't want to play anymore were to disappear?

2: IDENTITY: ARCHETYPES

The word "archetype" was coined by psychologist C. G. Jung and he believed they were narrative patterns that exist within the human psyche. He believed that these characters are present in all members of our species and throughout history, which is why we can see traces of them in art, literature, dreams, and cultures around the world.

An archetype is the core of your personality and is influenced both by your in-born nature and your life experiences. If your core archetype is "The Hero", you have a tendency to be courageous, but also to attract people to you who need "saving." It's like being cast in a movie as a "hero" and you're playing the part.

There are many archetypes, however Jung focused primarily on 12 that symbolize core human motivations. Below you will find a simplified description of each archetype. You may find that more than one feels like it represents a core part of your personality or identity, however there is usually one that makes you feel "yes, this is me!"

Also, your core archetypes can change over your lifetime. Identify if you feel a certain archetype represents who you WERE versus who you are NOW. Then, consider if you're hanging on to any of the beliefs from your old archetype, that no longer serve you now.

The Dreamer:

- Life is for: freedom and happiness
- Fear: being punished unfairly, being bad or wrong
- Strength: faith and optimism
- Weakness: naïve, defensive
- AKA: innocent, romantic, utopian, naïve

The Good Neighbor:

- Life is for: connecting to others, belonging
- Fear: being left out, different, standing out, rejected
- Strength: empathy, down to earth, peaceful
- Weakness: loses one's own self, superficial
- AKA; good old boy/girl, silent majority

The Hero:

- Life is for: proving one's worth, courage
- Fear: weakness, vulnerability
- Strength: competence, courage, boundaries
- Weakness: arrogance, always battling, attracts people who need saving
- AKA: warrior, dragon slayer

The Caregiver:

- Life is for: protect, care for, rescue others
- Fear: selfishness and not being needed
- Strength: compassion and generosity
- Weakness: martyrdom, self-sacrifice, being exploited
- AKA: altruist, helper, saint, nurturer

The Explorer:

- Life is for: freedom to discover yourself through exploring
- Fear: getting trapped, conformity, emptiness
- Strength: autonomy, independence, ambition, integrity

- Weakness: aimless, lack of commitment
- AKA: seeker, wanderer, individualist

The Rebel:

- Life is for: breaking rules, revolution or revenge
- Fear: powerlessness or complacency
- Strength: outrageousness, radical freedom, disrupting status quo
- Weakness: crime, conflict, instability
- AKA: revolutionary, wild, outlaw

The Lover:

- Life is for: intimacy, connection, relationship and being attractive
- Fear: being alone, unwanted, unloved
- Strength: passion, appreciation, connection
- Weakness: people pleasing, losing self in others, dependency, attention seeking
- AKA: friend, team-builder

The Creator:

- Life is for: creating things of enduring value, making visions reality
- Fear: mediocrity, settling, the status quo
- Strength: imagination, problem solving, action
- Weakness: perfectionism, impatience
- AKA: artist, inventor, innovator, dreamer

The Jester:

- Life is for: living in the moment
- Fear: being bored or boring others
- Strength: joy, levity, play
- Weakness: wasting time, irresponsibility
- AKA: the fool, practical joker, goof off

The Sage:

- Life is for: seeking the truth, growth

- Fear: ignorance, being duped or misled
- Strength: self-reflection, intellect, seeking knowledge
- Weakness: studying to excess with no action, over analyzing
- AKA: philosopher, advisor, thinker, teacher

The Visionary:

- Life is for: understanding the laws of the universe, making things happen
- Fear: unintended negative consequences
- Strength: following dreams, big picture, future vision, win-win solutions
- Weakness: becoming manipulative
- AKA: catalyst, inventor, charismatic leader, medicine man

The Ruler:

- Life is for: control and power, winning
- Fear: chaos, losing control, being controlled
- Strength: responsibility, leadership, organization, goal oriented
- Weakness: being authoritarian, unable to delegate
- AKA: leader, manager, aristocrat

3: BECOME WHO YOU WERE MEANT TO BE (YOUR LIFE PURPOSE)

Every human being has untapped potential. They are born with certain talents and traits, and their life experience teaches them skills and inspires passions within them. If you look back at the story of a person's life, it is often very clear that their life has been leading them along a pathway toward something—toward a higher purpose—a higher meaning for being on this earth.

Some people believe that our higher selves come to this life with a mission. Other people believe that we simply are dealt a hand and we have to decide how to play that hand. Regardless of what you believe, it is important to recognize that we all have the option to CHOOSE. We can choose to look for the deeper meaning in the experiences of our lives. We can choose to identify our talents and passions and make decisions to put them to work in our lives. We can choose to develop our potential and make our unique impact in the world.

In our Life Purpose course, we dive deep into a process for uncovering the deeper meaning and purpose in a person's life. Here we will look at the core of this process—talents and passions—which point in the direction of who a person is meant to be.

First, ask the following questions about childhood:

- What came naturally to you? What were you good at?

- What did you LOVE to do the most?

- What did you want to be when you grew up?

Then, ask the following questions about your earlier adult life:

- What do you wish you had done differently with your career or your life?

- What did you feel yourself drawn to over and over again?

- What did you used to do that you really enjoyed that you aren't doing any more?

Lastly, ask the following questions about your current life:

- What comes easy for you that may be hard for others?

- What have you become an expert at?

- What would other people say are your greatest qualities? Talents?

- What would you like to change in the world?

Looking at the answers to all of these questions, what does it seem like your life has been preparing you for?

What is your greater purpose?

4: BECOMING YOUR BEST SELF: HOW WOULD I NEED TO THINK AND BEHAVE?

After reflecting on the activities in this section, it's time to look at what it would take to be living in integrity with who you really are. How would you need to be thinking and behaving differently in order to bring your BEST self to life?

After evaluating the different roles you play (whether they're in your career, family, or elsewhere), which roles do you feel are the MOST important for you to change in order to fully embrace your BEST self?

For *each* role you wish to change, ask yourself the following questions:

- What needs to be changed about how I THINK about what this role is and who I am in it?

- What needs to be changed about my BEHAVIOR?

- Next, after looking at your talents and passions, what did you determine your life has been preparing you for?

- In what ways are you not currently living up to this greater purpose and mission in your life?

- How are you not using your potential?

- What needs to be changed about how I THINK about yourself, your life, and the gifts you have to offer this world in order for you to move forward in the direction of your greater purpose?

- What BEHAVIORS do you need to stop, change, or start in order to live in integrity with your best self?

- What things that you enjoy doing, are great at, and make you feel alive do you need to do more of?

- What are you passionate about that you want to spend more of your time focused on? How can you make your passions a priority?

- What do you need to learn more about or practice in order to use your gifts and go for your dreams?

This activity is meant to be a check-in point. In the next sections we're going to dive deeper into the thoughts and beliefs that may be holding you back from reaching your true potential, but then later in the book we'll be looking at what goals you want to set and work toward in order to create the lasting change that you're looking for. When you set any goal in life, always check in with what you've discovered in this section about who you REALLY are and the greater purpose and meaning in your life. You want every goal you set for yourself to be in integrity with your higher self, your best self. This is how not only you will be successful, but more importantly how you will find true fulfillment.

SECTION 6: DEVELOPING A MINDSET OF SUCCESS (GROWTH MINDSET)

1: THE GROWTH MINDSET

There is one core underlying belief that needs to be developed in order for true transformation to be possible—the belief that you CAN change your thoughts and behaviors.

If you don't believe you can change, you won't.

Two Key Underlying Psychological Principles:

1) Locus of control: what you believe is and is not within your control. Some people feel like life is simply happening to them, like they're a victim to whatever might happen. They have an external locus of control.

Other people believe they are in control of their lives. Even when something happens to them that appears to come from the outside, they still see how they have power over the outcome. This is an internal locus of control. How do you develop an internal locus of control and feel empowered about your life? That leads us to principle number 2.

2) Develop a bias toward action: If you feel like your life is out of your control, you're unlikely to take action because you don't believe it will make a difference. You have a bias toward inaction. So, in order to overcome this, you can begin taking action and seeing what happens. Doing this over time shows yourself that you have more influence over your life than you thought. You develop a bias toward action, meaning you believe you're the type of person who takes action to influence their own life. This, in turn, develops your internal locus of control and makes you feel empowered to direct your own life. It gives you confidence.

But, there is one core underlying psychological principle that is even more important to understand: The Growth Mindset.

People who have this mindset are:

- More resilient
- Better at coping with failure
- More likely to challenge themselves
- Those who do not have it are:
- Less resilient
- Poor at coping with failure
- Avoid challenge that could reveal their flaws

QUIZ:

Consider this example and how you would feel if it was you. Imagine that you had a terrible day. You spilled coffee on your shirt on the way to work, you got a parking ticket on your lunch break, and your boss reprimanded you for publishing a document with several major errors. How would you react?

a) You'd feel bad about yourself for being clumsy, unintelligent and unlucky. You'd accept that this is just how your life goes.

b) You'd be upset but you'd be thinking about how you should probably use a better travel mug, be more careful when you park, and double check your work.

Then, answer these questions:

If you were told that your intelligence, like an IQ score, is something about you that you can NOT change, would you:

a) agree

b) disagree

If you were told that talents are something you are born with (or without) would you:

a) agree

b) disagree

So, did you answer mostly a's or b's?

Before you dive into what this all means, the number one most important thing you need to know about it is: If you don't already have this mindset, you can LEARN IT.

This core belief system is called the Growth Mindset. And the opposite way of viewing the world is called the Fixed Mindset.

If you answered all b's, you have a growth mindset. If you answered some a's, that's okay, because your answers to those questions will be very different by the time you finish this book!

Growth Mindset

The growth mindset is a belief that your basic qualities, including intelligence and talent, can be cultivated through effort. This means that while people may be innately different, with certain aptitudes and temperaments, all aspects of a person's abilities and personality can be changed, regardless of where your setpoint is.

Fixed Mindset

The fixed mindset, on the other hand, is a belief that these same characteristics are fixed at birth or become locked-in by a certain age. This means that some people are just inherently more talented or intelligent than others and that's just the way it is.

If you feel like at least part of you believes that intelligence and talent are fixed, you are not alone. Most people, especially in the western world, believe this because our culture teaches us that it's true. SO, it's not your fault. Emphasis is put on testing us to determine our intelligence, such as taking an IQ test or being graded. No one stops to think that a single test taken on a certain day at a certain age cannot possibly predict how well you would do on the test years later, after learning more, or when you're in a better mood. But, we're taught that these tests identify what we've got and that's it. We're stuck with it.

We also live in a culture that is obsessed with "natural talent". There are 2 problems with this.

1. The people who work hard to develop their abilities far out-win the naturals in the long run.
2. If being a natural is so important, it actually discourages the effort it takes for those who have to work at it.

And, that's exactly what happens.

People with a fixed mindset believe they'll always have the same level of talent regardless of how much effort they put in. They've either got it or they don't. Because of this the spend a lot of effort trying to prove their abilities and intelligence. They want to look smart. So, if they're not immediately good at something, they stop doing it. This is because they're in a constant quest to prove that they are talented or intelligent. To a fixed mindset person, effort is a bad thing. Having to work hard at something is a signal that you're not a natural talent or that you're not of high intelligent because if you were you wouldn't' have to try. As a result, they don't challenge themselves, they don't like trying new things, and so they never develop their potential. They're trapped reaching only as far as their current abilities can take them. They're trapped because failure is devastating. It means they are a failure. And because they don't want to have to take on an identity as a failure, they'll often blame others or the outside world. Fixed mindset people find joy in being the best or being judged as talented or smart.

Growth mindset people see the world very differently. They believe that the more effort they put into something, whether it's practicing or learning, the better they will become. If they're not good at something they see it as a sign that they have to work harder. They have little need to prove they are talented or intelligent and instead are on a never ending quest to continue to grow. How hard someone tries is how they measure the person's value. They enjoy challenges and see them as an opportunity to learn something and expand their boundaries. They may not like failing, but they don't ever believe they are a failure. They see failure as a learning experience. Growth mindset people find joy in progress and learning.

So, what is important to know here is that if you didn't already know that you can change and improve your talents, skills, intelligence, characteristics, and behaviors, now you know!

2: THE LOCUS OF CONTROL

When we try to create a new story, one of the most important things is to focus on the things that we can control. Too often we waste time and energy on things that are outside of our control and influence, when we could be spending it on creating our new story. In fact this, is why many people never create their new story—they are focused on changing the wrong things. We need to direct our focus on things we CAN control—things within our "circle of control".

There are 3 levels of influence:

1. Things that you can directly control
2. Things you can influence
3. Things that you have no control and influence. So let us look at those things.

Things you can control:

It's important to recognize that our perception of what we can control strongly influences what we do and what we feel about situations in our life. The perception of how much control you have in your life is called "Locus of Control." We've included a quiz that will help you identify how much control you feel that you have.

A person who has a predominant internal locus of control believes that they can (or should be able to) influence all of the events and outcomes in their life. On the other hand, someone who has a predominantly external locus of control tends to blame the outside world for nearly all things that happen in their life. As you can probably see, being at the extreme end of both of these tendencies can have a negative impact on your life. For example, someone with a high internal locus of control tends to blame himself or herself, and beat themselves up, when something does not go their way, even if they had no control of the outcome. In other words, it is important to recognize they there are things that we do not have control over. On the other hand, someone with a high external locus of control tends not to take responsibility for anything, blaming everyone else for things that are clearly within their control. They don't take control of their life because they do not think that they have the power to make the difference. People with a balanced locus of control have a realistic view of what they do have power over.

Below is a small list of things that you do have control over right now:

- How much effort you put into something
- How many times you smile, say "thank you", or show appreciation today
- How well you prepare for something

- How you react to an emotion (yes, you have a choice)
- What you focus on
- How you interpret a situation
- What you commit to doing or not doing
- What conversations you have and what you engage in
- How much you focus on the present moment
- What you tell yourself and how nice you are to YOU
- How you take care of your body
- How many new things you are exposed to
- What you do in your free time
- Whom you spend your time with and who your friends are
- What information you consume: books you read, media you listen to or watch
- When you ask for help
- Whether you make plans and act on them
- How much you believe what other people say
- How long it takes you to try again when you fail

This is just a small list of examples. However, notice that all of these items are DIRECTLY related to YOU. Yes, YOU, your actions, thoughts, emotions, beliefs and choices are what are within your circle of control.

Remember that some of the things that you have control over have consequences, but those consequences do not take away from the fact that you have a choice.

What are things that do you have control over that you would want to change and take charge of?

How will taking control help you create your new story?

Things you can influence:

Outside of your circle of control, the next level is your sphere of influence. Our influence and perceived influence is critical to our wellbeing. In fact, researchers, Dr. Sommer and Dr. Bourgeois have been able to show that the more influential you feel you are, the greater your happiness and wellbeing. This is because feeling that we influence others gives us a sense of purpose, meaning, and control. Notice that influence is different than control. Influence does not mean telling people what to do or making them do something. That does not lead to happiness. And, the truth is that you CAN'T make people do anything.

There are two ways that you can increase your level of happiness when it comes to our influence.

1. **Increase your influence on others around you.** The type of influence we're talking about here is being a leader in our inner circle—meaning leading by example. For example, when we follow our dreams, stand up for what we believe, and when we grow, we empower other around us to do the same thing. It is about living in the reality that if you change your behavior, or attitude, other people tend to notice and are affected by those changes whether they want to or not.

2. **Increasing your awareness of how you currently influence those around you.** When you acknowledge the positive impact you are having on others, it boosts your confidence.

Influence is a normal part of human nature. It's up to you to decide in what ways you are influenced by others and whether you are a good influence on those around you. The sphere of influence goes both ways because the people that you may have influence over also influence you. Choose who you are around wisely, and be aware of the impact you have on others.

Make a list of those closest to you whom you influence over and/or who influence you:

- How do you influence them (both negative and positively)?

- How can you become a better positive influence on them?

- How do they influence you (both positive and negative)?

- Are there any negative influencers that you can replace with positive ones?

Becoming a positive influencer will increase your happiness and wellbeing. Living your new story will serve as an empowering example for others. But, keep an eye out for the negative influencers in your life that may hinder the story that you are trying to create.

3: YOU CAN CHANGE YOUR BRAIN

Everyone knows that when you lift weights repeatedly over time, your muscles grow bigger and get stronger. And, when you stop exercising the muscles, they shrink again and get weaker. Most people don't know that when they practice any activity and learn new information, their brain changes and gets stronger, much like a muscle.

Understanding Neuroplasticity and Why It Matters

The brain is made up of billions of tiny nerve cells called neurons that all connect together through a network of over a trillion tiny branches (made up of dendrites the receivers, and axons the transmitters). Every time we think or act, it is because these neurons are communicating by sending signals through their dendrites, all the way to whatever locations are needed to trigger the cells to act. The signal itself is a chemical called a neurotransmitter. These signals are responsible for every step you take, for your heart beating, and for thoughts and emotions.

You may have heard the phrase "neurons that fire together, wire together". What this means is that certain neurons connect to each other through chains in the network or pathways from one area of your brain to another. When you use a certain pathway or "wire" repeatedly, the connection between the neurons strengthens. The process is called myelination and it literally involves growing a protective coating that encases the wire like the rubber coating on an electric wire. This myelin sheath makes signals able to move faster, which the brain loves because it's primary goal is efficiency.

So, when you repeat a behavior, an action, an emotion, or a thought over and over again, the pathway responsible for sending the signal becomes stronger and it becomes easier and easier. This is how skills are developed and habits are formed. It's also how emotional triggers are created and negative patterns are formed. Whether the outcome is good or bad, whatever that you do repeatedly changes the physical workings of the neural connections in your brain.

But, interestingly, scientists have found that because of this process the brain literally grows bigger, just like a muscle—not in size but in weight.

And what's important to know is that for many years scientists believed that the brain loses its ability to grow and change early in life, but they now have proof that even old brains can change by developing more connections and strengthening wires.

The Truth about Smart and Dumb

Most people believe that everyone's intelligence is fixed. You're born smart, dumb, or average and your capacity for learning is determined by what you're born with. But, interestingly no one thinks babies are stupid because they can't talk or read or solve equations. Those things, of course, are all learned with practice and exposure. And, babies can't walk until their muscles get stronger. We don't question this, but somehow, we've been tricked into believing that after a certain point, you're either smart or not and that's the end of it.

But, the truth is that, while there are minor variations between people with innate predispositions, the factor that contributes to a person's level of intelligence at any age is their exposure to information and experience combined with the amount of time they spend learning.

The truth is that intelligence can be grown just like any physical capability can be improved. It takes work and it can be challenging, but this is also the case for a weightlifter who wants to increase their strength or a runner who wants to increase their speed.

So, now you know that you can change and grow your brain. When you practice a new skill over and over again or you increase your exposure to new experiences repeatedly, your brain grows stronger in those related areas. People who play an instrument have increased brain activity in the area of their brain related to their hands. People who drive cabs have a larger hippocampus than everyone else, which is the area of the brain responsible for spatial memory. So, whatever you spend more of your time and energy doing will grow your brain in the corresponding area. But, it's not just repeating something that makes you learn and grow, it is DELIBERATELY learning how to get better at it. What unlocks the door to true growth is learning a new tool, strategy, or insight that helps you do something BETTER—not simply doing more of the same old thing.

And that's why, in this book, we're going to provide tools, strategies, and insights for changing your thoughts and behaviors. You'll develop your awareness of the thoughts and emotions that go on in your mind and body. You'll learn strategies for recognizing patterns and identifying underlying beliefs that influence what you think and do. You'll learn how thought works and what's going on inside your brain and body when you experience emotions so that you can understand how these thoughts and feelings cause you to behave the way you do.

The human brain is the most amazing and powerful tool in the world and you are blessed to have one. It may not have come with an owners' manual, but now that you know how it works you have the power to use this tool to change your life.

4: COMMON MISPERCEPTIONS ABOUT THE GROWTH MINDSET

When learning about the growth mindset for the first time, there are several common misperceptions that can prevent you from being able to develop a true growth mindset, either because you reject the idea because you feel like having a fixed mindset makes you wrong or bad or because you struggle to identify authentic growth mindset from simply the appearance of it.

First, no one is either 100% fixed or 100% growth oriented. Everyone is on a spectrum between the two. In addition, someone can be fixed in one area of their life, such as believing their intelligence is fixed, but have a growth mindset in other areas, such as believing they can develop their singing ability.

Second, people's life situation can impact how they view themselves and others. For example, you could have a growth mindset that help you achieve success within your organization and then be promoted to leadership position and then start believing that you have all the answers and fall into a fixed mind set. More than anything, it's important to know that everyone's mindset changes over their life.

Third, being positive or open minded does not mean someone has a growth mindset. Also, people who learn about a growth mindset who lean more toward a fixed mindset may try to take on qualities they believe growth mindset people have, even thought they are still seeing from a fixed perspective. It's important for fixed mindset people to remind themselves (or for you to remind them) that it takes practice and time to learn a new way of viewing the world. There is nothing wrong with them, in fact, it's extremely common! But, the good news is that they can change.

Fourth, it is easy to get the idea that growth mindset people don't care about outcomes, only effort. But, it's not that positive outcomes are not valued or rewarded, it's that the effort is valued and rewarded more. And, effort that doesn't eventually lead to progress is not rewarded either. The goal is learning and progress, not just effort. Effort that doesn't result in progress over time is wasted effort. If a low performing employee is not learning from their mistakes, even after support, they may not be a good fit for that position.

5: DEVELOPING A GROWTH MINDSET STEP 1: AWARENESS

Now that you know what a growth mindset is and why it is such an important belief system, you can begin to practice this way of thinking.

Awareness of Your Self-Talk and Fixed Mindset Triggers

Everyone has an internal voice, and part of this voice is an inner critic, inner hater, or inner doubter—it is the fixed mindset persona. You can hear this persona within the negative self-talk that happens in your thoughts and mind. It can sound like:

- I'm not good enough.
- I will probably fail.
- I can't do this.
- I don't want to risk it.
- I shouldn't have to try so hard.
- If I'm not naturally good at this, I should just quit.
- It's not my fault.

- This makes me uncomfortable, I'm not doing it.
- Why try if it won't change anything?

What does yours often sound like? (Circle the ones you relate to or write your own below.)

Give your fixed mindset persona a name.

Naming it helps you remind yourself that this mindset—or habit of thinking—is not who you are!

I will call my fixed mindset persona: _____

Identify your triggers.

What situations tend to trigger your fixed mindset persona?

- When you're thinking about taking on a big challenge or learning something new?
  ___always   ___ sometimes   ___never
  What does your fixed mindset persona tell you when you're in this situation?

- When you're thinking about making a change?
  ___always   ___ sometimes   ___never
  What does your fixed mindset persona tell you when you're in this situation?

- When someone criticizes you?
  ___always   ___ sometimes   ___never
  What does your fixed mindset persona tell you when you're in this situation?

- When you fail at something?
  ___always   ___ sometimes   ___never
  What does your fixed mindset persona tell you when you're in this situation?

- When something goes wrong? Do you beat yourself up or blame someone else?
  ___always   ___ sometimes   ___never
  What does your fixed mindset persona tell you when you're in this situation?

- When someone else makes a mistake? Do you judge them?

Criticize them?

____always   ____ sometimes   ____never

- What does your fixed mindset persona tell you when you're in this situation?

- When you're under pressure or on a deadline?

  ____always   ____ sometimes   ____never

  What does your fixed mindset persona tell you when you're in this situation?

- When you procrastinate or are feeling lazy?

  ____always   ____ sometimes   ____never

  What does your fixed mindset persona tell you when you're in this situation?

- When you have a conflict with someone?

  ____always   ____ sometimes   ____never

  What does your fixed mindset persona tell you when you're in this situation?

- When your reputation is at risk or you worry what others will think?

  ____always   ____ sometimes   ____never

  What does your fixed mindset persona tell you when you're in this situation?

6: DEVELOPING A GROWTH MINDSET STEP 2: PERSPECTIVE

You may not always be able to change what happens around you, but you always have a choice of how you respond, react, and how you view the situation.

- When you catch your fixed mindset persona with a limited thought, ask yourself, what else might be going on here?

- What is a more realistic and optimistic way to look at this situation?

- What are the good aspects of this situation?

- How can I look at this differently?

Here are examples of rephrasing fixed mindset thinking as growth mindset thinking. Be on the lookout for any time you hear your fixed mindset persona taking over your internal dialogue, such as the reactions to the triggers you identified or the following common fixed mindset thoughts, you can change your perspective to a growth mindset,

- When you hear yourself thinking something like: "What if you're not good enough? You'll be a failure."

    Change it to: "Everyone starts out not being good and successful people all fail along the way."
- When you hear yourself thinking: "If it's this hard, you're probably just not good at it."

    Change it to: "If it's hard, it means I need to put in more effort and it will be a great achievement when I get good at it."
- When you hear yourself thinking: "If I don't try, I can't fail and I will keep my dignity."

    Change it to: "If I don't try, I have already failed and I have no dignity."
- When you hear yourself thinking: "It's not my fault."

    Change it to: "If I don't accept whatever part of this is my responsibility, I give away my power."

Go back through the fixed mindset triggers you identified and what your persona tends to tell you and rewrite a NEW thought from the growth mindset perspective.

- My fixed mindset trigger thought:

- My replacement growth mindset perspective:

- My fixed mindset trigger thought:

- My replacement growth mindset perspective:

- My fixed mindset trigger thought:

- My replacement growth mindset perspective:

- My fixed mindset trigger thought:

- My replacement growth mindset perspective:

7: DEVELOPING A GROWTH MINDSET STEP 3: ACTION

So, at this point you've noticed your fixed mindset persona thinking limited thoughts and you've changed your perspective. The next step is the most important, and in fact is what truly makes someone have a growth mindset. The most important factor for developing a growth mindset is action. Ask yourself these question whenever you find yourself facing a challenge and hear that doubting fixed mindset voice discouraging you.

- What did you learn from the experience?
- What could you do differently next time or going forward?
- What would help you achieve this goal that you haven't tried?
- What do you need to learn or what information do you need to gather?
- What steps will you take?

DON'T STOP THERE! List out the steps that you will take, and for each one, identify exactly WHEN you will do it. If anything on your list cannot happen within 1 week, save it for later and re-assess at the end of the week. For everything else, include when you will do it and what you need in order to do it.

Lastly, take 5 minutes to visualize yourself taking each of these steps, as you imagine they will play out, including achieving the goal and outcome you are aiming for.

Practicing a Growth Mindset

Select your favorite affirmations from the list below or write your own and put them somewhere you will see them every day, such as next to your bed, on your mirror, on the cover of your day planner, attached to your computer screen, or programmed into the calendar of your phone to remind you to look at them every day, at least once.

- Everyone has a fixed mindset to some degree. Now that I know the difference and I know I can change, I am developing a growth mindset.
- Challenges, risks, and failures do not reflect that I am a failure, they are opportunities for me to grow and improve.
- I care more about the process and the journey and who I become

71

along the way than I do about the outcome.

- I am glad that I am not perfect and that I never will be because it means I am not limited to where I am today.

- What other people think about me is none of my business. I no longer allow other people's opinions and judgments to hold me back from living a life of fulfillment and reaching my potential.

- I am always looking for the meaning and lessons contained in all situations that can help me fulfill the greater purpose in my life.

- I move past the discomfort of making mistakes quickly because I learn the lesson and allow it to help me improve so I can do better next time.

- I know that no one starts out great at something and so I am willing to try new things and practice skills I would like to have, putting in the time and effort I know it takes to master this area.

- I am the master of my thoughts, emotions, and actions and I do not give my power away by reacting to others criticism, judgment, or actions in a negative way.

- Having to exert effort in order to be good at something is a good thing because it shows me that I am capable of learning and improving. I love knowing I am not limited to my current strengths.

- I love knowing that even if someone else may be more naturally talented in an area than I am, a person with better work ethic will out perform a person with talent every time.

- I know that most truly successful people have failed their way to success.

- I have skills and knowledge today that I didn't have before because I learned and grew in those areas, so I know I can develop any ability I want.

- If my talents, abilities, and intelligence are not fixed, this means my potential is truly limitless!

- Write your own:

*See Developing Self Efficacy Add-on/print at attached to workbook next. *

SECTION 7:
SELF-MASTERY:
TRANSFORMING FROM
WITHIN

1: THE 3 IRRATIONAL BELIEFS AT THE CORE OF YOUR SUFFERING

You have probably gathered by this point in the book that it is not the situations in our life that make us miserable, it is the way we think about the situations that determines how we feel. So, why do we assign meaning to life event in the way that we do? The full answer is complex and could fill the pages of another book. (In fact, we have another book called the Human Mind Owner's Manual that dives deeper into how our minds, thoughts, beliefs and emotions work!) The short, yet profound, answer is that all of our pain and suffering is caused by 3 core irrational beliefs.

Not all people hold the same variation of these beliefs, but we all believe them in one situation or another and these beliefs are always irrational. These beliefs are like internal rules that we have for how we, others, and the world "should" behave. The problem is that we normally are not aware that we have these beliefs. And if we do catch ourselves thinking these things, we don't normally question them.

By identifying which of these core irrational beliefs you tend to fall into the most, you can begin to become aware of the situations in which you apply these bogus rules. You can look out for these beliefs in the stories you tell about yourself, others, and your life throughout this book, as well as notice yourself thinking this way in your every day experience. Below you will find a description of the 3 beliefs, as well as additional details that will help you identify if this belief is active within you. We'll also address the emotional and behavioral consequences for continuing to hold onto these irrational beliefs, as well as present an alternative belief to practice when you catch yourself reverting back to these old, irrational rules.

BELIEF #1—APPROVAL: I must be approved of by others to be worthy.

- Need: acceptance, belonging
- Fear: judgment, rejection
- Demands: I expect myself to perform well and win approval from all significant others at all times, and if not I am a failure, unworthy, and deserve to suffer.

Symptoms:

- Places unrealistic expectations on oneself
- Over-concern with what other people think
- Achievement and popularity determine self-worth
- Self-critical, lack of self-acceptance

Emotional Consequences

- Depression, feeling not good enough, unable to express or embrace true self
- Anxiety, worry about what others think, being judged
- Low confidence, feeling bad about yourself, others disapproval means we are bad, can't be yourself
- Behavioral Consequences
- Risk-avoidance, for fear of being judged for failing or being different
- Shyness, for fear of being embarrassed
- Procrastination, for fear of failure, judgment, risk
- Unassertiveness, for fear of rejection or criticism
- Workaholism, in order to gain approval

REPLACE WITH THIS RATIONAL BELIEF:

I have value as a human being simply by being my authentic self, and I desire love only from those who appreciate me and recognize the good in me.

BELIEF #2—JUDGMENT: Other people must do "the right thing" and meet my expectations in order to be worthy.

- Need: importance, superiority
- Fear: unfairness, disappointment
- Demands: expect all significant others to treat you kindly and fairly, as well as act appropriately, and if they don't they are unworthy, rotten people who deserve to be punished

Symptoms:

- Unrealistic expectations on others, including expecting them to be infallible, perfect
- Assuming you are the sole authority on what is right and wrong
- Assuming you have authority over others
- Believing everyone else is responsible for catering to your needs

Emotional Consequences

- Anger, rage or fury when others intentionally or unintentionally treat you poorly or unfairly or don't meet your expectations
- Impatience with others who make mistakes or aren't perfect
- Bitterness against others for not meeting your needs
- Resentment toward others for being imperfect and especially for treating you unfairly or not meeting your needs

Behavioral Consequences

- Aggression and violence as a way of punishing others for being inappropriate or not meeting expectations
- Bigotry and intolerance of anyone who does not meet your definition of right and wrong
- Bullying others to enforce your belief of the way others should behave or be
- Nagging others to elicit the right action you expect and require

REPLACE WITH THIS RATIONAL BELIEF:

All people, including myself, are imperfect, have value to offer, and have a unique perspective of the world.

BELIEF #3—COMFORT: Life must be easy, without discomfort or inconvenience.

- Need: certainty, comfort, justice
- Fear: adversity, uncertainty, discomfort
- Demands: expect all external conditions to be pleasant and favorable at all times and when they're not it is awful and unbearable.

Symptoms:

- Unrealistic expectations about life being perfect
- Belief that living a trouble-free life is a birthright
- Lack of belief in your ability cope with adversity
- Complete rejection of all life problems as unacceptable

Emotional Consequences

- Low frustration tolerance
- Self-pity and "poor me" attitude
- Depression, hopelessness
- Discomfort anxiety

Behavioral Consequences

- Procrastination
- Shirking
- Drug and alcohol abuse
- Overindulgence in "feel good" behaviors (e.g., overeating)

REPLACE WITH THIS RATIONAL BELIEF:

It is perfectly natural for life conditions to not be ideal or perfect and it's okay if situations do not exist the way I would prefer because I am capable of finding solutions to problems and making changes that bring me happiness and opportunity regardless of the situations that happen around me.

2: BANISH APPROVAL-SEEKING AND SAY NO TO "SHOULD"

One of the 3 core beliefs is about the need for approval, and it leads us to judge ourselves and try too hard to gain approval of others. Approval-seeking is one of the most detrimental forces that leads a person to live inauthentically and out of integrity. Instead of making decisions based on what is best for them and instead of honoring who they truly are, they live their life for others—constantly adjusting themselves to be what they believe other people think they SHOULD be.

This approval-seeking behavior is so common that we don't even notice we're doing it. Some people have been people pleasing so long they don't even know who they really are. For me (Natalie), my approval-seeking behavior started in 5th grade when a boy at my bus stop told me "Natalie, you always act like an animal." The truth is he was probably right. But form that point forward I was always concerned about not looking weird or being judged. Of course, that didn't stop me from being weird because I couldn't help it, and it didn't stop me from being judged... I was made fun of and bullied for many years.

For many people, the approval-seeking behavior starts with their parents. Their parents might be controlling and critical. They may also send mixed messages, for instances telling their child to choose what they want to wear, but then when the child makes their choice, the parent tells them their cloths doesn't match and make them go change. Constantly having their own preferences questioned or criticized leads to a child who, when asked by the store clerk, would you like a lollipop, the child looks at the parent, not because they're looking for the parent to give them permission, but to see if they even want the lollipop at all. They lose their ability to think for themselves. This, unfortunately, follows many people into adulthood.

There are a number of common approval-seeking behaviors, including:

- Changing your opinion at the first sign of disapproval
- Feeling anxious when someone disagrees with you
- Being unable to say "no" and so doing things for people and then resenting them for it.
- Being susceptible to sales people and tending to buy thing you don't want
- Apologizing all the time
- Faking knowledge about a topic in order to impress others

If you relate to any of these things, you are not alone! In fact, approval-seeking is one of the most common afflictions! We all want approval and belonging. But, the problem comes when we don't just want people to like us, we demand it. We NEED it. If you simply want approval, you're happy when people like you. But, when you NEED it, you feel like you're going to die if you don't get it. Not only is this a problem because it is inevitable that not everyone is going to like or approve of you… but, it's also a problem because it pushes you away from your true self.

Believing you NEED approval is like saying "your view of me is more important than my own opinion of myself." You sacrifice yourself for the opinions of others.

Think for a moment about a time when you were really upset that someone didn't agree with you or like you or approve of what you did. And now ask yourself, how would your life actually have been different if the person DID approve? In most cases, the truth is it wouldn't have made you any better off.

One of the areas where many people, especially women, tend to become preoccupied about seeking approval from others is how they look. People spend an absurd amount of money and time buying cloths that others view as "name" brand or high-end, cutting and dying and extending their hair, having fake nails installed, filling a closet with shoes, and painting their faces with makeup. Not to mention plastic surgery. When asked, many people say the reason they do it is because it makes them feel better about themselves, more confident. They want to look good. But, what does that really mean? How does having perfectly quaffed hair, eyelash extension, and $200 shoes actually make you a better person? Why would it make you more confident? You guessed it, because of what you believe OTHER PEOPLE will think about you because of it.

So, the question is, how would other people's approval or envy actually impact you? Does some random stranger looking at you and thinking you look sexy or rich actually mean anything? What would happen if they didn't think you looked great? How would that matter? Actually, if you think about it, in most cases you don't even know if anything thinks you look great because they don't say anything. And then, when they do say something, often you're annoyed or offended! How much sense does THAT make?

How much energy to you spend wishing you were thinner, more muscular, had better skin, had better hair, had less of a neck glottal, had that new pair of shoes everyone wears these days? Would any of that really matter?

And if not, isn't there something else MUCH MORE worthy of your time?

Now don't get me wrong, I think it's a great idea to seek approval of your behavior in the sense that you want to be a kind, considerate person and for people to recognize that. You don't want to denounce approval of others as an excuse to be a jerk and be like "I don't care what you think." But, at the same time, you don't want to be a doormat and bow down to everyone else's desires and demands just so that they think you're nice. Be a good person, but honor yourself first.

The best way to decrease your approval seeking behavior is to practice getting other people out of your head. What I mean by that is to pay attention to the thoughts going on in your head, especially the ones that tell you what you should and shouldn't do.

When you tell yourself you shouldn't do something usually that "should" was told to you by someone else. So, whenever you hear that word "should" it's a sign that you're thinking someone else's thought or believing someone else's belief. The solution is to stop "shoulding" on yourself. Banish the word "should" from your vocabulary. When you hear that voice in your head urging you to do something because you "should", ask yourself:

- Why should I do (or not do) this?
- Who told me I should?
- Do I truly believe I should?

In some cases it will genuinely be something that you agree you should do 100%. In that case, make it a MUST for yourself and do it!

In most cases you'll recognize that you DON'T really believe you should do it and that you're only trying to make yourself d oit because someone else's voice is in your head telling you should. Even if it's not a specific person, in general you are seeking to do what you should in order to gain approval.

It's a bad habit, so be on the lookout for the world SHOULD and question any belief that is attached to it. Then, make your decision based on what YOU truly believe. When you do you'll be living in integrity with the true you.

3: QUESTIONING BELIEFS AND EXCUSES

A belief is just a thought you keep thinking. They are habits of thought that we think automatically about aspects of life because we assume they are true. It is important to question your beliefs because the truth is that just because you believe them doesn't make them true. You probably used to believe something that you don't believe anymore. That's good news because if some of what you believe is limiting you, you can change it!

First, you have to identify what you believe. Then, you'll look at where the belief came from, whether or not you know for sure it is true, and the impact it has on your life. In another chapter we'll look at how to change these beliefs.

The beliefs you're going to be identifying include everything from what you believe failure means, to your beliefs about money, career, and what it means to be a man or a woman, and more.

For each, ask yourself how you expect that they "are," "should be", or what they "mean". *Answer each quickly with your FIRST inclination.*

What is your belief about this prompt?	Where did the belief come from?	Is it true? How do you know?	How does it negative-ly impact your life?	What would you like to change it to?
Failure means:				
Experiencing challenges means:				
Other people are:				

Money is:				
Work is:				
A career should be:				
The future is:				
Education is:				
Emotions are:				
Being a parent means:				

Being a child means:				
Being a man means:				
Being a woman means:				
Being single means:				
Being married means:				
Friendship means:				
Health means:				

The beliefs that can hold a person back the most are excuses. Excuses are beliefs people hold about why they cannot do what they really want in life. Most people don't question their beliefs or excuses. They might believe these limitations are true, but the truth is that in most cases they are simply excuses. The truth is that it is often easier to continue to tell yourself that something is not possible for one reason or another than to actually have to face what it would take to make the needed changes.

So, the best way to stop these limiting beliefs from holding you back is to question them. The problem is that you might not be aware of these limiting beliefs because they seem so normal and they happen automatically. So here is what to look for. Pay attention to any time you catch yourself saying something such as, "I really wish I could do this, but I can't because…". The key word to look for is BUT. When you say you want something BUT… whatever reason you give that comes after that "but" is the excuse.

So, like the last activity, once you identify the excuse you're going to question it.

- Is it true?
- How do you know?
- What does this excuse give you an excuse for avoiding?
- How can you challenge this belief?

Then, replace the excuse with a good reason why you CAN do it.

Here are several common excuses, including the truth that challenges them. Evaluate these beliefs for yourself and see what other excuses you tend to use so you can question them and empower your beliefs.

- **But, I'm not good at it.** You're not good at it because you haven't practiced it! You're probably keeping this excuse around because you're afraid of failure. (See the Growth Mindset section (6) for help with this one.)

- **But, people won't like/approve of me.** You are not living life for anyone else. Sometimes you have to embrace the pack of haters if you want to live your dreams. You're probably keeping this excuse around because you're afraid of being judged. (See the 3 Irrational Beliefs section (7) for help with this one.)

- **But, it's too hard.** How would you know; have you done it? It's only too hard if you don't know how to do it. The good news is you can try it and learn. You're probably keeping this excuse around because it gives you an excuse not to try because it's not possible. (See the Growth Mindset section (6) for help with this one.)

- **But, it's too risky.** There are no risky changes, only risky people. If you prepare yourself, you can minimize risk. You're probably keeping this one around because if you don't take the risk you cannot fail.

- **But, it'll take too long.** What is a "long time" anyway? If it is going to take 5 years, won't you be 5 years older whether you do it or not? You probably use this excuse to avoid having to make a decision or a commitment.

- **But, it costs too much.** Now this not true in most cases. Chances are you are spending a ridiculous amount of money on something you don't need, like coffee, cigarettes, clothes—everyone has something they could give up to fund their dreams. Besides, everyone is capable of generating money with a side gig. Get creative! How COULD you afford to do this?

- **But, it's overwhelming.** If you are feeling overwhelmed it's because you are trying to "bite of more than you can chew." You can't eat a big meal all at once. Make a plan for how you're going to get where you want to go but then focus on one thing at a time.

- **But, I don't have time.** This is the most commonly used "but," and it is totally bogus. The truth is you are wasting time every day on unimportant things. Make it a priority and you will find the time.

- **But, it's not possible:** Has anyone else accomplished it? Yes. Are they imbued with magical powers? No. We've heard so many times people who say "I've tried everything" but when asked what they tried the truth was that they tried the same two things over and over and gave up. The people who have accomplished what you want to do got there by doing something different than what you are doing. First of all, they tried. Second of all, they kept trying new things. And third, they learned what they needed and never gave up.

So, what other excuses do you tend to tell yourself? What other reasons do you hold yourself back?

The purpose of this activity is not to negate the challenges you face in your life, but it is meant to challenge you to stop simply assuming your limiting beliefs are true. There may be obstacles that have to be worked around, but they are not there to stop you, they are there to inspire you to get creative and commit to living your best life no matter what. We'll end this chapter with one of our favorite quotes

"If you don't go after what you want, you'll never have it. If you don't ask, the answer is always no. If you don't step forward, you're always in the same place." — Nora Roberts

4: CHANGING LIMITING BELIEFS USING THE TABLE LEG METHOD

Imagine your belief is like a table-top and the evidence that supports your belief is like the table legs. You look at the evidence and make a conclusion—a belief about it. Just like with a table, if you knock enough legs out from under it the belief will collapse. You do this by creating doubt about your evidence or looking at it in a different way. Then, after you collapse the old, unwanted belief that makes you doubt yourself or your dream, you can use the same method to build up a new one. That's right, it works in reverse! If you determine a belief that is more empowering that you'd prefer, you can find evidence that SUPPORTS your new belief. Add at least 3 legs and the table will stand.

For example, if you believe that you are bad at math, you may have several reasons for this belief. First, it seems to run in your family. In fact, your mother said it's in her genes. This plants the first seed. Then, in 5th grade you got a math answer wrong when you were asked to do the math problem on the board in front of the class. It was embarrassing and reinforced your belief, making you think, "geeze, I guess mom was right!". Then, you failed the last two tests you took in your high school algebra class. You felt bad about it. Now the belief is stuck.

But, believing that you are innately bad at math will hold you back. First, because you expect to do poorly you'll be more nervous when you take math tests, you'll be less likely to try harder or practice since you believe you're simply unable to do math. You will unintentionally prove yourself correct. This is called a self-fulfilling prophecy. In the end, you'll avoid things that you might have enjoyed simply because you expect they'll involve math and you don't want to do it because you think you're bad at it. Maybe you love science but you never pursued a career in science because you didn't think you could do the math. Maybe you wanted to start a business but didn't think you could handle the finances because of your math deficiency.

When we hold limiting beliefs, they hold us back from our potential.

The good news is even the more strongly held beliefs that hold up the overall belief can be undone. The key is to question the evidence we use to support it, remove the superglue, and find a new, more empowering belief to replace it with.

Before we begin, it's important to understand that when we're talking about limiting beliefs, we are not saying that the belief is FALSE. It may be true or based on things that really happened. But, whether it's true or false isn't the point. We're looking at beliefs that are either empowering or disempowering. They're either useful or harmful.

5 Step Process for Changing Limiting Beliefs

STEP 1: Identify a limiting belief you would like to change:

Make a list of all of the things you can think of that provide evidence (table legs) that support your belief (at least 3 pieces of evidence).

STEP 2: Identify an alternative belief that is more empowering:

If you're having a hard time identifying a more empowering belief, ask yourself "what if I believed the opposite"? You want to choose a new belief that is believable. So, instead look for an IMPROVED belief. So, that could be "there is always opportunity in the market if you provide an exceptional product or service."

STEP 3: Unstick the emotional superglue:

Sometimes we become emotionally attached to our limiting beliefs. We experience benefits or emotional payoffs for keeping our limitations around, which makes them sticky. It is like supergluing the table legs to the floor. So, ask yourself: what is the emotional payoff for holding onto this belief?

Be honest with yourself. Write down everything you can think of that may be an emotional or practical benefit.

Next, ask yourself: do these benefits outweigh the costs of keeping this limitation? __Yes __No

- If your answer is YES—that the emotional payoff is worth it—then you will most likely NOT be able to change this belief because you are too attached to it.

- If you answer is NO—the payoff is NOT worth continuing to be limited by this belief—well, then it's time to celebrate because you've just dissolved the superglue! You actually WANT to change, and that means it's time to start dismantling that table.

STEP 4: Create doubt by reframing your evidence:

Like we said, you believe what you believe because you look at the evidence and come to a conclusion. But what if the evidence was wrong, incomplete, or you just weren't seeing it clearly? That would make you question your conclusion, and that's exactly the point of this step. For **each piece of evidence** you identified for your limiting belief, ask yourself the following questions:

- Could this be untrue?
- Is there more to the story?
- What is an alternative explanation?

The point is to question the evidence enough to create doubt. Some evidence will be harder to refute than others, but that's okay as long as you can knock out enough to leave less than 3 legs standing!

STEP 5: Find evidence to support your new belief:

Now we're gong to flip this around and build up the supporting evidence to solidify your new belief. Looking back at your desired belief, make a list of everything you can think of that supports this new belief. You only need a minimum of 3 but you want to create as many legs as possible so that this believe is way stronger than the old, limiting one.

With enough supporting legs, your new belief will stand. It might not be as strong as your old belief at first, but that is okay.

In many cases, the table legs that held up your old belief may have been really thick or really superglued because of the emotions tied to them. When thinking about evidence for your new belief, it may be harder to find emotionally-charged evidence, so you want to think of as many things as you can. The number of supporting legs will make up for the less powerful examples.

You've done it! You changed your limiting belief and replaced it with a new empowering belief! But that doesn't mean that the old limiting thoughts won't pop back up sometimes. You may need to remind yourself of this new belief multiple times, or even read it to yourself regularly, but through repetition you will be able to banish that limiting belief for good!

5: DEVELOPING AWARENESS OF EMOTIONS

The skill of emotional self-control is perhaps the most valuable skill you can EVER acquire.

Sometimes people have a difficult time identifying their emotions and it's usually because of one of the following reasons:

- We were made to think our feelings don't matter
- We were made to fear expressing our emotions
- We were made to feel guilty if our emotions (or desires) were an inconvenience on others
- We were discouraged from feeling or expressing specific emotions

Because of our conditioning, some people stop expressing their emotions and often repress them (hold them in). Other people go a step further and stop allowing themselves to have them. In either case, this can lead to a lessened ability to recognize how they feel.

Even people who did not learn to repress or turn off certain emotions—even if they feel things deeply—they can simply not have ever been taught about their emotions and so they cannot clearly identify them.

If you want to re-gain your power to direct your own emotional state, you need to be able to:

- Notice you're experiencing an emotional state
- Identify what it is
- Know what to expect
- Know how to influence a new emotional state

Emotional States

Emotional States are actually 2 different things:

- The STATE is the physiological "feelings" that you experience
- The EMOTION is the psychological interpretation or "label" you put on the state

We experience complex states made up of chemical and hormone interactions that cause a variety of reactions in the body. Our emotions are the interpretations we make of these experiences—or the labels we give them.

So, based on what we talked about in Thoughts Create Emotions, we need to add a couple steps to the process.

Situation → Interpretation (thought) → State → Interpretation (label) → Emotion

What this means is the body responds to the thought first, then our minds interpret the reaction, label it, and an emotion is born.

We can have physiological feelings that aren't emotions. We can feel hot, cold, nauseous, or energetic. But, when we interpret them to have meaning, we turn them into emotions.

Emotions literally mean action: e-MOTION. Each emotional state is designed to get us to do something, and often we do. Our emotional state affects our behavior, but it does not cause it. When we're angry we're more likely to be aggressive, but our cognitive (thought) processes allow us to make those decisions.

The Map is Not the Territory:

The labels we give emotions are like a box or a map. What's printed on the box may signal what's inside, but it is NOT what is inside. Just like a map may describe a territory, however it is NOT the territory. Maps are simplified, inadequate and ultimately flawed. It would be like eating a menu. In the same way, what we call "anger", the word, is not the experience. Saying you "love" someone hardly does the experience any justice. In fact, all words are simply signposts pointing toward meaning. The word "tree" is not a tree.

So, what IS an emotion if it's not map? Well, it's not a "thing" either. You see, labeling an experience as an emotion makes it seem like a NOUN. This is why many people believe emotions are things they HAVE or that happen TO them. The truth is that emotions are verbs (emoting is the verb)—they are a PROCESS. Fear is the process of fearing, which is a string of sensations that occur in a pattern. Fear takes many steps from observation or contemplation to processing and interpreting; then to physiological reaction and FEELING, and finally labeling it as fear.

If you obscure the process underneath a word label, you end up believing that emotions aren't under your conscious control. Once we recognize anger is a process, we recognize we have power over it.

Emotion Identification Chart:

On the next page, your will find 6 common emotions and descriptions of the emotion, physiological state, and common resulting behaviors. This chart will help you get a general idea of the signs and symptoms of each emotion to make them easier to identify; specifically, easier to identify early. Keep in mind everyone experiences each emotion somewhat differently and you may not experience all of the characteristics.

LABEL	EMOTION	STATE	BEHAVIOR
Happiness	Intense, positive feelings of well-being, pleasure, contentment, delight, joy, optimism, and gratitude. Affirmative, positive thoughts and mental clarity.	Head held high (posture), wide-eyed, smiling, laughing, relaxation of muscles, open body language.	Pleasant voice, friendly, swinging arms, dancing.
Boredom	Low-intensity, unpleasant feelings of apathy, restlessness, indifference, emptiness, and frustration. Defeatist thinking or wishing things were different.	Low energy, slumped posture, smirk or frown, low eyes, shallow breathing.	Resting head, fidgeting, staring.
Anxiety	Vague, unpleasant feelings of distress, uneasiness, stress, apprehension, and nervousness. Thoughts of uncertainty and worry, racing thoughts, difficulty concentrating and remembering.	Restlessness, sweating, clammy hands, hunched shoulders, swallowing, quickened breath, darting eyes, butterflies in the stomach, nausea.	Pacing, biting lip, fidgeting. Irritability, hyper-vigilance.

Anger	Intense, uncomfortable feelings of hostility and hurt. Feeling out of control. Thoughts of blame and resentment. Difficulty thinking clearly or rationally.	Muscle tension, headache, tight chest, increased heart rate, increased blood pressure, heavy breathing, clenched fist, furrowed brow, showing teeth, clenched jaw, sweating, trembling, flushed cheeks, large posture.	Loud voice, yelling, cursing, sarcasm, pacing. Sometimes leads to aggression, including hitting a wall, throwing an object, or lashing out at a person.
Sadness/ Depression	Feelings of intense pain and sorrow, guilt, unworthiness, disappointment, helplessness, gloominess, loss, grief, numbness, meaninglessness, loss of interest. Defeated thinking and difficulty concentrating and remembering. (Depression is a long-term period of sadness.)	Slumped posture and hunched shoulders, long face, slow movements, pouting, body aches, crying, shaking, crossed arms, fatigue, upset stomach, monotone voice.	Curling up into a ball, laying around, withdrawing, irritability.
Fear	Intense feeling of dread, impending doom, or panic due to a perceived danger or threat. Paranoid or worst-case thinking and hyper focused on the object of the fear.	Increased heart rate, increased blood pressure, alert eyes, high eyebrows, corners of cheeks pulled toward ears, clammy, sweating, quickened breath, goose bumps, butterflies in the stomach, shaky voice.	Freezing, fleeing, hiding.

Practicing Emotional Awareness and Identification

Next time you catch yourself experiencing an emotion that is distinct, ask yourself the following questions. Practice this line of questioning often, especially when experiencing unpleasant emotions.

- How do I feel?
- How do I know?
- What do I feel? Sensations?
- Where do I feel it? Locations?
- Where in my body did it begin? Move to?
- How do I recognize when OTHERS experience this emotion?
- Do I notice any of these signs in myself?
- What do I observe in my body language, vocal tone, thoughts, behaviors?

6: AFFIRMATIONS, INCANTATIONS AND THE POWER OF YOUR NAME

Affirmations

There is a power of your words. We are always affirming something about ourselves and what we believe about our capabilities. This can be positive or negative. We can tell our selves that we are terrible at something and that we have a terrible memory. So what happens we live to that reality because we tell our brain that its our reality. Why because when our statements direct your FOCUS toward what you want. This triggers your Reticular Activation System (RAS), which is a small section of your brain that tunes in your awareness to stimulus in your environment that is a match for what you're focused on. We are exposed to a million bits of information at any moment and we are only consciously aware of 2,000 of them. If you're thinking negatively, you notice negative things. If you're thinking about red cars, you're going to see them everywhere. If you're thinking about how to get new contracts for your photography business, your ears will pick up the conversation in the adjacent aisle in the store where someone is talking about their upcoming wedding.

Therefore, our words also knows as affirmation are a powerful force. So if you don't know what affirmations are they are written or spoken positive statements that, when consistently practiced, rewire our thoughts and beliefs (and therefore emotions).

If you have a negative belief (or common thought) that causes you to feel bad, you can replace it with an empowering thought. If you repeat it to yourself regularly, such as when the negative belief is triggered AND at pre-determined times of the day, you practice this new belief, helping it become ingrained into your implicit, automatic, memory. Over time this thought becomes habituated and you BELIEVE it.

4 Keys to Successful Affirmation Statements:

1. It must be believable and within your control
2. It must be present tense (happening now), personal (I), positive (no "not" or "don't")
3. You must FEEL IT
4. You must repeat it REGULARLY (3-5 times per day for 21-30 days)

What is a belief that you hold or a negative thought you say to yourself regularly that you would like to REPLACE with a more empowering, positive affirmative statement?

Write a NEW phrase to replace the old one, using the guidelines above. Repeat this affirmative statement at least 3 times a day (5 to 10 times each session). Consider posting it on your mirror, computer or nightstand where you can see it regularly. Do this with additional beliefs/thoughts.

The Power of Your Name

Another key that people miss is the power of your name. You see, when the brain hears your name it triggers your mind to tune-in and place importance on whatever comes after your name. So, if you say an affirmation using your name it makes it more powerful. For example, after failing my (Joeel) first year of college, I read a book that talked about affirmations. I started looking at my self in the mirror and saying "Joeel, you're a genius" among many other statements. I went back to school and graduated with a 3.8 with my bachelors, 3.9 with my masters, and PhD with a 4.0. Did my intelligence level change? No. It was my belief in myself through my statements.

Incantations

Incantations take affirmations a step further and make them PHYSICAL. An incantation is a phrase or language pattern that is said out loud and with an engaged physiology. Putting affirmations into motion engages more of your brain and makes it more real.

Incantations are also spoken OUT LOUD. This also sends additional signals to your brain that you are SERIOUS. If you must do your incantation when other people are around and you don't want to draw undo attention to yourself, you can do it silently—but whenever you can, say it out loud.

Incantations can be a whole phrase like an affirmation, or they can be a short phrase such as "I am confident!"

What affirmation would you like to use as an incantation? Or, you can write a new one.

What movement could you make while reciting this incantation? (Examples: Raise your hands in the air like you're cheering, pull in your elbow as if you're saying "yes!", jump up and down or dance.)

Next, pick a certain time that you will practice your incantation EVERY DAY. Be specific so that it's easy to habituate it. For instance, you can do it right after you brush your teeth.

7: REFRAMING YOUR THOUGHTS

It truly is not what happened in your life that creates your story, it's how you INTERPRETED (or framed) your experiences.

The Power of Interpretation (Perspective)

Your interpretation of events either empower you or disempower you. Even the worst experiences of life, that feel like a curse, can be re-framed to find the silver lining or blessing contained within them. It is the MEANING we attach to a situation that determines whether it moves us forward or holds us back. The meaning also impacts the way we react and feel about any circumstance.

Find the Silver Lining

For every seemingly negative circumstance in life, there either was (or could be) a positive outcome because of it.

You can choose to interpret events in a way that is DISEMPOWER-ING (makes you feel resentful or guilty) or you can interpret them in a way that is EMPOWERING by asking yourself:

- "What else might be going on here?"
- "What did I learn from this experience?"
- "What can I do differently next time?"
- "What positive outcome eventually came as a result of this situation?"
- "What meaning does it have? What purpose does it give me?"
- "How can I use this for GOOD?"

Make a list of any experiences from your life story (past or present) that are "negative" and then identify the positive outcomes and/or the empowering perspective you can take from them.

You'll dig deeper into this in the coming chapters about change.

8: CULTIVATING MINDFULNESS

"The outer situation of your life and whatever happens there is the surface of the lake. Sometimes calm, sometimes windy and rough, according to the cycles and seasons. Deep down, however, the lake is always undisturbed. You are the whole lake, not just the surface." — *Eckhart Tolle*

For most people, the chaos and noise happening around them and within their own minds feels like all there is. They live in a constant state of reactivity, being pushed and pulled by the thoughts and emotions they experience. They're controlled by a voice in their head that worries about everything that can go wrong, criticizes them for everything they do wrong, and feels guilty or angry about everything that went wrong. This voice interprets every situation instantaneously and we don't question it, just like we don't question our breathing. It all happens unconsciously, meaning we are unaware of it. And then we feel and act based on the voice's interpretation.

The truth is that everyone has a voice in their head, including you. Some people's voices are nicer than others, but everyone's voice tends to have the same disfunctions. But the good news—perhaps the best news anyone can ever hear is that this voice is not who you are.

For some of the people reading this book, you already know this well. For others, it may be the first time you have heard it, or the first time you truly understand it. If you've ever argued with yourself over something or you've ever noticed yourself thinking about something ridiculous or you've ever talked to yourself in your own mind, then you've experienced that there are two of you. There is the one that does the thinking, feeling, and reacting and there is the one that is aware of the thoughts, emotions, and reactions. You are that awareness. You are the presence that witnesses the voice, but you are not the voice.

Knowing this allows you to observe what your inner voice is doing and thinking. This is called self-observation or self-awareness. As you become more and more aware of what has always been going on unconsciously, beneath the surface of your awareness, you become conscious. You wake up from the dream. And the process for developing this awareness is called mindfulness.

Until you develop self-awareness and mindfulness, you will likely live much of your life on auto pilot, feeling like you have little control over your thoughts, emotions, or life. The truth is that unless you know what you're thinking, feeling, or doing, you have no way of changing it.

Simply developing this awareness is the key that unlocks all of your power. Power to direct your own inner voice, choose better-feeling emotions, and making better decisions.

Start by listening to the voice in your head as often as you can. Pay particular attention to any thoughts that repeat. Be the observer of what is happening inside of you—both the surface of the lake and the depths. See if you can find and feel the deep calm at the bottom of the lake even when the surface is rough.

As you practice mindfulness and observing your thoughts and reactions, you'll be able to recognize even more clearly that the presence doing the observing is the true you. When you notice yourself feeling angry, you'll observe that the angry part and the part observing it are not the same thing. This is important to know because your true self never becomes disrupted and entangled in these surface level dramas. There is a part of you that is at peace, content, safe, and joyful no matter what is going on around you and in your mind. Your higher self is untouchable, un-disruptable. Knowing it is always there means you can seek to find it in any moment.

And, just like when the sun dips below the horizon you know that it still exists, even though you cannot see it, this calm, peaceful presence that is you is always there, even if you cannot see it.

As you begin to pay attention with a sense of curiosity to discover what your inner voice is up to, you'll begin to notice interesting things it does. You'll notice when you are behaving in a way that is in alignment with our goals and our values, and when you are not. You'll notice when you are smiling even though you are actually sad, or when you say you are fine even though you are not. You may notice you are pretending to be mad when you really aren't, just to manipulate someone else's behavior. Or, you may notice that you are thinking negative thoughts about yourself, making you feel insecure. You may even notice when we are soothing yourself or feeling relaxed or happy.

The last thing you need to know about cultivating mindfulness before we move on is that the doorway to all awareness is the present moment.

Most people's minds have a strong habit of spending a lot of time thinking about the past or imagining, and usually worrying about, the future. But, the power to observe and redirect your thoughts, emotions, and behaviors is only accessible when you are focused on the present moment. When you're paying attention to what is going on in this moment, you can notice the mind remembering an experience from the past or worrying about the future. But, if yourself to go with your mind TO these past or future places, you lose your sense of awareness. For this reason, one excellent way to develop mindfulness and self-awareness is to pay attention as often as you can to what is happening RIGHT NOW. Pay attention to each step you take, to the noises going on around you, to your breathing. Once you pull your awareness back into the present moment, it gives you an opportunity to notice what you're thinking.

It is also important for you to know that the next time you notice yourself experiencing a negative thought or emotion, it doesn't mean you've failed—it means you've succeeded! Until you are able to become aware of these negative experiences you have little power over them. So, every time you notice a negative thought, celebrate! Give yourself a high five! Because now you know that this negative thought is NOT who you are. You are the one in charge and you will be spending the rest of this book learning how to develop this awareness and use proven tools to change the content of your inner world.

Notes:

SECTION 8: PREPARING TO SUCCEED

1: IDENTIFYING POSSIBLE ROADBLOCKS

When working toward a goal or creating life change, it is inevitable that there will be roadblocks and setbacks along the way. There is a saying that goes, "when human makes plans, God laughs." Point being, it is not going to all unfold perfectly. There are two keys to overcoming barriers:

1. Being preemptive and preparing for possible problems
2. Develop an attitude of flexibility and creativity

So, first, let's look at what barriers are likely to come up. It's important to understand that some of these issues may be practical, but primarily obstacles that hold people back are internal. That's why we spend so much time focusing on developing empowering mindsets and beliefs.

By identifying what might go wrong, you can prepare in advance, both with action and with mental preparation. Let's take a look at the most common roadblocks and how to overcome them.

Practical Things that Could Go Wrong: Considering your specific situation, what are some things that might go wrong? Think of as many things as you can.

Solution: Plan in advance whenever possible. Identify what you could do in the even that this happened, as well as anything you could do to prevent it. The trick to overcoming obstacles is to be prepared. Plan these action steps into your overall planning.

Frustration/Impatience/Disappointment: Because of the inevitability that something is going to wrong, you are likely to experience negative emotions, such as frustration, impatience, or disappointment. These are, of course, completely normal emotional responses, but the key is to not allow them to stop you from moving forward.

Solution: Be flexible. Set realistic expectations. Accept that it is normal for things not to go exactly the way you want. Allow yourself to feel what you feel, but then take steps to find a better feeling perspective of the situation. Look for what can be learned. Explore other options.

Resources: Sometimes there may things you need, that you do not have, in order to accomplish what you're trying to do. These can be physical items, financial resources, access to space, or even an environment that supports your decisions.

Solution: The solution here is resourcefulness. If you don't have what you need, get creative with your ideas for how to get it. Plan in advance for what you are going to need. Ask for help. Brainstorm ways to generate extra money to fund what you need to do.

Other people/Support: The truth is that our changes impact other people, and often they don't like it. Other times, when we make changes and go for our dreams, it threatens other people's limiting beliefs about themselves, and they react with doubt or criticism. Because of this, there may be people who try to dissuade you from doing what you are doing. It may be challenging to find support. And it may be challenging to do what you know is right for you when you know it will make other people unhappy or they will judge you.

Solution: In the event there is a practical problem that your decisions will cause with other people, plan in advance for how you will handle it. In most cases, however, the issues with other people are actually internal— you simply don't like how you feel knowing other people don't like what you're doing. But, it is important to remember that you have to put the oxygen mask on yourself first. If you live your life according to other people's desires you end up burnt out and empty with nothing left to give. Also see the Social Influences and Saying No lectures. At the same time, if you are seeking support you may need to look outside of your immediate circle.

Time/Organization: One of the most common barriers is time. In the Questioning Beliefs and Excuses lecture we address that not having time is an excuse, not a true reason not to do something. While it may be true that you have a lot on your plate and many responsibilities, including work, school, or family, however there is always a way to find the time.

Solution: First, it is important to understand that time is mental concept more than a practical unit of measure. What keeps someone from having the time to do something is a lack of prioritizing it, not a lack of time. At a practical level, you can find the time by evaluating all of the activities you do throughout the day and considering what you could eliminate that is less important than this thing you wish to do. For most people, this includes things like watching television and social media. It may be different for you. Also, planning in the actions you need to take to accomplish your goal is vital. If you leave it up to chance, without a plan, it is not going to happen. See the Creating Change Practical Steps section.

Motivation/Confidence: The most detrimental internal obstacle for most people is lack of motivation and follow through, which in most cases stems from a lack of confidence that they are going to be successful.

Solution: The most important source of motivation is a strong, clear understanding of why you are doing something, which is addressed in the "Big Why" lecture. It is also vitally important to understand that you cannot create lasting change if you are depending on feeling motivated. Motivation is an emotion that comes and goes. Creating a concrete plan helps you stay on track even in those moments when you're not feeling motivated. Confidence comes from a belief in yourself that you are capable of learning and growing in whatever ways are necessary in order to achieve your goals, which is addressed in the Success Mindset section as well as the Developing Change Confidence lecture. By working on mindset and confidence, motivation is increased. Combine that with commitment to a concrete plan, and you have a recipe for success.

2: WILLPOWER, CUES & TRIGGERS

Many people want to make changes to their fitness or eating routines, but the truth is it can be hard to not go back the old patterns and habits. Many people think that they should have the willpower to make the changes. However, willpower alone—self-control, resisting temptation—doesn't work. Our brain works with triggers and cues and these make it hard for us to make changes when we are constantly trying to fight the brain on what it has already learned it should be doing. This is why we have to build our willpower muscle. However, it is also important to recognize that we have to help our willpower because it is not usually enough. For example, researcher and psychologist Dr. Roy Baumeister has demonstrated that to build our willpower muscle we first have to develop awareness of things we want to change and then develop strategies for minimizing the cues that trigger the brain, making willpower challenging.

It is important to minimize cues and trigger when you are making any life change, but especially when the changes being made are related to eating and exercise because they are so habituated. If we don't do the work upfront to minimize the triggers that keep us continuing our current patterns, these cues in our everyday environment will pull us out of any new behavior we initiate.

Don't leave it up to willpower: It is important to recognize that willpower is like a muscle, and that if we over rely on that muscle we may find it harder to resist triggers and therefore fail to create change. Dr. Roy Baumeister, a psychologist at Florida State University conducted studies on decision-making and willpower and concluded "self-control is like a muscle and that if you over exert the muscle it gets tired." You can try to will yourself to make changes, but temptations will drain you and make it harder for you to be able to make long-term changes.

Build Your Willpower Muscle

The willpower "muscle" is just like any other muscle—when you give it regular workouts, it grows stronger. The problem is that most people believe that willpower is that in-the-moment feat of self-control against an overwhelming craving or temptation. Exercising your willpower does not mean flexing your ability to torture yourself by sitting in front of warm, off-limits brownies. It does not mean telling yourself you are going to quit smoking and then hang around smokers at lunch. This does not work. True willpower comes when preparation meets commitment.

So, now let's look at how to exercise your willpower muscle:

Commitment: Make a clear-minded decision regarding what you will or will not do, based on a clear understanding of why you want to do it and what will happen if you don't.

What have you decided you will or will not do?

Preparation: You cannot expect yourself to be able to resist temptation in the moment. Instead, identify what you need to do in order to be prepared! Answer the following questions:

- What do you need to do to be prepared?
- Do you need any materials or equipment?
- Do you need to change your schedule?
- Do you need to remove anything from your home?
- Are there scenarios or locations or people you need to avoid or be prepared to face with a pre-determined statement of why you will or won't be doing something?

For example, if you want to utilize your willpower to stop eating chips, throw out any that are in your home and commit to not buying any more. If you want to do 100 sit-ups every morning, don't leave it up to how you feel in the moment—instead, set an alarm reminder, put your matt in the right position the night before, and commit to do it when the alarm goes off, NO MATTER WHAT.

Regularly practicing different types of self-control: It has also been shown that if you practice self-control on smaller things it will build your willpower muscle. Identify simple things you can do to practice your self control. For example, waiting to check your social media, portion control on unhealthy snacks, keeping a food dairy, not responding to someone's comment that triggers you emotionally, sitting up straight, or any other thing that will help you to practice self-control

Visualize it: Mentally project yourself into the future—into a situation that is a trigger. Imagine the trigger happening but rather than imagining you responding like you normally would, instead imagine responding with the desired behavior. Practicing this mentally gives the brain a new framework. Once you can break a pattern in your mind you'll be better able to break it when you are exposed to the trigger in real life.

3: THE 3 R'S OF HABIT CHANGE

Habits are our driving force in fact most of our habits are unconscious and are triggered by our environment. The brain is creating to be efficient, so it develops patterns. In fact, 50% of your daily behaviors are unconscious. Habits are any pattern of behavior or routine. They are our unconscious programming. Your habits shape your life as your daily behaviors are basically a sum of your habits. How happy you are, whether you reach your dreams or goals, or your mental state among other things are a result of your habits. Therefore, if you want to improve anything in your life thank you must change your habits. In the last chapter, we talked about eliminating the need for willpower by eliminating the triggers in your environment that keep you doing the old patterns and habits that you no longer want. Now we're going to talk about how to create POSITIVE habits and patterns.

So how do you do that? Well research on human patterns has shown that there are 3 steps to habit change and formation. So, whether the habit is good or bad they follow this pattern. These patterns of change come from Psychology professor of Stanford BJ Fogg and other research in the field of psychology.

The 3 R's of Habit: the Loop

1. **The Reminder:** All our habits have triggers and these triggers initiates the behavior.
2. **The Routine:** This is the actual habit, action, or routine that you have.
3. **The Reward:** Is the benefit that you get from the actual behavior. Keep in mind that even negative consequences have benefits and serve as a reward.

The first step is to identify what habit, behavior pattern, or routine you want to eliminate, replace, or create.

If your goal is to stop an unwanted habit, one key is to replace it with a new habit. So, first identify the undesirable habit, and then determine how you could replace or shift the habit.

For example, you may wake up in the morning and you see your phone and it serves as the trigger for you to follow your habit of checking your social media. You are rewarded by the social interaction, especially the links and positive comments, which trigger dopamine in your brain. In fact, social media is created to be addicting, to meet our basic human needs (but for that we would need a totally different book). In order to stop this habit, you would need to replace it with something else you do immediately upon waking up. One idea is you could have an MP3 player next to your bed with a song that inspires you that you can listen to first thing in the morning. You *could* have this song on your phone, but the problem is it may be too tempting to just sneak over to the Facebook page and take a quick look. In fact, it's probably a good idea to keep the phone away from your bed.

Another example there may be a specific person that you tend to have conflict with. When that person calls you, it triggers a feeling of tension. You then pick it up and have a conversation with them that creates stress (habit). The reward is the drama since it releases adrenaline which is very addicting. Now, it might not be possible to eliminate contact with this person, so in order to change the pattern you will need a different way of dealing with the phone conversations. For instance, you could program a photo to pop up on your phone when the person calls that softens your feelings toward them. You could choose not to answer it and instead call back after you've gathered yourself and can go into the conversation with a positive attitude.

So, once you decide your replacement habit or you identify a new habit you want to create, use the 3 R's of Habit Change.

Step 1: Set a Reminder for Your New Habit

Keep in mind that willpower is ineffective long term since our brain and memory works with triggers. Therefore, if you think you just must just be motivated to create change you may find that it is ineffective and that you will fail to create new habits. Keep in mind that our behaviors and patterns are mostly unconscious. Therefore, a reminder serves to pull us out of our unconscious mind and pattern to consciously make a new behavior.

Of course you can literally set yourself a reminder, such as an alarm on your phone, if the habit you want to create is something you could do at the same time every day (or throughout the day).

If you're replacing a habit, you would do the new habit at the same times you normally would have done the old habit.

But, if you're starting something new that wouldn't fit with a literal reminder, you can piggy back off something else you already do on a routine basis, using it as a trigger for the new habit.

For example, you could put a note in the mirror in the bathroom (which you will look at every morning) that reminds you to run through a list of at least 10 things you are grateful for.

Or, if you want to meditate everyday then you may tie it into your morning tea that you already drink. So, after drinking your tea meditate for a specific amount of time. The tea will be your trigger.

So, what are some simple healthy daily habits that you already have that you do every day?

How could you integrate your new habit into one of them?

Step 2: Make it a Routine

Ritualize a new habit through planning and scheduling. If your new habit will take 30 minutes every day, block it out on the calendar for the same time every day and make it nonnegotiable. The less you have to think about it, the easier it will be to do. If you have a routine and you do it consistently, you will easily become habituated. The reality of life is that if you don't plan it you won't do it. This is, again, why using the piggy-back method is so effective—because you're it's easier to add something new to something else you're already doing something routinely.

If your new habit is something you need to schedule in, where and how are you going to set aside time for it?

What else do you need to prepare in advance so that you have every-thing you need at the scheduled time to get up and go?

Once you create a routine, protect it.

Even well-established habits or routines can get thrown out the window when the pattern is disrupted. For example, people who exercise daily can fall out of habit when they go on a vacation for a week. One option to protect the routine is to continue to exercise while on vacation, keeping the timing similar if possible. Alternatively, they can recognize that they'll need to plan ahead to re-instate their routine and can sign up for an exercise class or make an appointment with a personal trainer for a day or two after they return home. They can also set reminders or leave themselves notes inspiring them to get back into their pattern.

Step3: Create a Reward

Some new habits will have a natural rewards built in-- for example, telling yourself the things that you are grateful for in the morning will reward you by helping you feel happier and put you in a state of gratitude to start your day. Other new behaviors may not have such an immediate reward, therefore developing a reward is important. For example, they did a study where they had people go for a jog in the morning. A part of the group could eat a small piece of chocolate after their jog while the other group had no reward. So, what they found was that the people that ate the small piece of chocolate ended up jogging significantly more every morning for that 30-day study. More importantly when they followed up six months latter they found that those that had the chocolate maintained their new habit significantly more than those that did not.

So, think about what you could do to reward yourself for your new, positive habits. What are some ideas of things you could do to reward yourself every time you do the desired behavior? Keep in mind it can be as simple as simply taking a moment to affirm yourself and give yourself a high-five.

What are some ideas of things you could to to reward yourself for meeting certain milestones? (Such as every time you make it a week performing this new habit, you give yourself something special, whether it's something you do that you enjoy or a small gift to yourself.)

4: EMBRACING UNCERTAINTY: FREE YOURSELF, EXPAND YOUR BOUNDARIES

Escape from Darkness

When I (Natalie) decided to Florida from New Hampshire when I was 23, everyone I told responded with pessimism and discouragement. "You'll be back." "It's too hot down there, you're going to roast." "There are old people everywhere." "The water at the beach gets so warm it's not even refreshing." "I've heard the traffic is TERRIBLE." Everyone had negative things to say. Everyone except one guy who responded more honestly. When I mentioned I was moving to Florida he paused for a moment, reflectively, and said "I wish I had the balls. I've always thought about moving south to get away from these horrendous winters, but the truth is I'm just too much of a chicken."

I thanked him for his honesty and told him what I had just realized in that moment—that most of the rest of the people I'd told, who had reacted with negativity, had probably also always thought about moving south but that, unlike him, they couldn't face the truth.

The truth is that they avoided acknowledging their desire for a better (or at least warmer) life out of fear.

They limited themselves to avoid the discomfort of change. So, my brazen and abrupt move to the other side of the country—without a job or a house or a nest egg—threatened the tightly held belief they clung to that it wasn't possible. It might have been a little crazy, but it was definitely possible.

After the winter we had just experienced—with practically zero snow and temperatures so cold they close the schools for cold—the only thing I saw as "crazy" was living through another year in a frozen hell.

Hunger for Light

I distinctly remember the moment I made my decision. It was February, and the little snow we had was melting and a patch of brown and crumpled grass was showing through. I saw a small green sprout reaching toward the sun. I empathized with it's hunger for the light. I felt compassion for the months it had spent trapped beneath the frozen earth. I felt the relief of breaking through. I realized it was not the plight of the sprout I was empathizing with, it was my own.

*"Never again," I said to myself in that moment. And I meant it.
Fear of the unknown or not, I was not about to submit myself
to further torture within a self-inflicted boundary of a state.*

I arrived in Florida on April 1st, but I can assure you it was not I who was the fool. 13 years later, I'm still here. I live at the beach. And all of those people's fears were totally bogus, especially the one about the warm water. 88 degree Gulf Beach water is like a saltwater spa. It is heaven. Stop lying to yourself!

Mental Boundaries

So, the other day I was in the Florida Keys celebrating my birthday with my husband and daughter on a snorkeling trip. On my way there, we stopped to visit family, and at our hotel the attendant asked where we were from and what we were there for. When we said we lived 4 hours away and were heading to Key Largo, he mentioned that he'd always wanted to go to the Keys, but that anything over an hour away is too far. From the hotel, Key Largo was little more than 90 minutes south.

*I thought to myself, "too far for what?" For experiences
worth having? For opportunities and beauty and adventure?
For life to exist?*

It reminded me of the limited mental boundaries that I once held for myself. You see, after moving to a giant state like Florida I realized that most people in small states develop what I call "small state mentality". For some reason, there seems to be a psychological boundary around the literal boundary of one's home state. For whatever reason, it feels weird to cross it. In Florida, I found myself driving 3 or 4 hours away without questioning it, which I found odd because when I lived in New Hampshire it felt absurd to drive to Boston, which was only an hour away. New York City (2 states away) was only 4 hours away, yet I never would have thought of going. My loss! But, in Florida, you can drive 8 hours and still be in Florida.

This hotel attendant reminded me that it isn't just people who inhabit small states who develop this mental boundary—it's everyone—except other people's boundary is a certain driving distance. It seems so normal for me to drive long distances to experience places I'd like to go that it always surprises me when I meet people who live out their lives within an hour radius. For some, it's a 20 minute radius.

I find it creepy. Even creepier are the people who live within their radius in the same town they grew up in. Eeek. I simply cannot imagine living such a limited life.

Self-Imposed Limitations

These mental physical boundaries are a perfect example of self-inflicted limits. Whether it's a state or a certain distance from home, these boundaries are ultimately meaningless. I challenge you to ask anyone (yourself included) what reason they have for not wanting to go beyond whatever boundary they've set for themselves, and I assure you there will be no reason. What could the reason possibly be? Sitting in a car is too painful? Slight discomfort or boredom are simply too much to bear? Their brain will explode if they drive too far? They have an irrational fear of being chased by rabid baboons? WHAT IS IT?!

The only legitimate reason I can think of is that they fear that they may experience something beyond that boundary that challenges their belief that their life is what they want and that everything they could ever need or love exists within a 20 minute radius

What's your boundary? 20 minutes? 60? 4 hours?

What about with regard to your job? Will you only work somewhere within 20 minutes of your house? It's understandable if you don't want to waste your time commuting, but what if your absolutely ideal dream job was 45 minutes away? Would enjoying what you spend 8 hours a day doing be worth spending an extra hour on the road? Or, what if you are happy with your job but your dream beach house became available at a price you could not refuse. Would it be worth driving an hour each way to spend your time at home listening to the waves lap upon the shore, watching the sunset, and swimming when you want to?

It's a toss up... you have to choose between your *time* and the *quality* of how you spend your time. Or, you can completely re-think the whole thing, like I did, and create your own job and work from home at the beach.

The truth is that you have a choice but that you don't allow yourself the full range of options because you create imaginary boundaries of limitation. Stop it!

Excuses are Choices

I didn't spend a couple days on vacation in the keys because I have the money and flexibility to do it. I have the money and flexibility to do it because long ago I made a decision to expand my boundaries. At a time when my peers were settling in with their small state mentality and setting up lives that operated within a 20 to 60 minute radius, I was driving across the country with all of my possessions and cat it tow. At a time when money was tight, I prioritized experiences over disposable pleasures like Starbucks, clothes and useless possessions. At a time when most young adults were climbing the bottom rungs of their chosen career path of stability and comfort, I was cliff diving into a path of entrepreneurship and it's resulting uncertainty and freedom.

I'm not saying I think there is anything wrong with being happy with where you live and living a simple life. I'm just saying that it's one thing to stay living in your home town, but it's another thing to NEVER leave it. I think people don't explore because they fear that life beyond their chosen boundary may reveal what they may be missing out on.

Lack of exposure to the outside world is the best way to ensure you never question the authenticity of your satisfaction with your life.

I understand... humans are comfort-seeking beings. We want life to be pleasant. But, we try so hard to control the world around us that we limit it to only what we know. But, then within that narrow path of certainty we make ourselves miserable. The monotony of our mediocrity highlights every slight disruption. When every day is like the one before we seek the variety and novelty we crave through conflict, drama, or substance abuse.

Ask yourself, have you lived 20 years of life, or have you lived 1 year 20 times?

If this sounds like you, I'm going to tell you the one thing you've been trying to avoid hearing... that you have a choice. Every day since the beginning of your chosen limitations, you have had a choice to be different. You have always had the option to cross the boundary, move it, or demolish it. And, every day going forward you will still have this choice. You can say yes to life. You can get in the car and drive farther than ever before. You can sit down and think about what you really want, but that you've told yourself you cannot have... or cannot go... or cannot do. You can spend your money differently. You can spend your time differently. You can stop hiding behind comfort and conformity and obligation.

And, if you're one of those people who loves your home town and wants to raise your kids and grow old where your roots are planted, do it! Every community needs established families to keep tradition and culture alive. But, don't do it out of fear or obligation.

Many people use this famous quote, by George A. Moore, as an excuse to stay put:

> *"A man travels the world over in search of what he needs
> and returns home to find it."*

To which I reply: *Sometimes.* More often, those who explore find themselves and what they need and love through exposure to people who think differently than they do, through finding beauty and meaning in experiences and places they didn't know existed. The truth is most people who leave don't return home. And those who do return home and find that, after all, what they always wanted was right where they began... they first had to "travel the world over" in order to realize it... or at least leave their state!

You've never heard anyone say "staying within a 1 hour radius was the greatest decision I ever made."

Take the risk. It's the only way you'll ever know that the only true risk is staying stuck where you are... in the prison of your own making. Only you hold the key. You always have. It's time to stop limiting yourself with imaginary boundaries.

You're free to go.

SECTION 9: THE PSYCHOLOGY OF CREATING CHANGE

1: DEVELOPING CHANGE CONFIDENCE: THE CHANGE RESUME

The change guarantee: from this situation, something good will come.

This powerful activity will help you provide EVIDENCE to yourself that you CAN do it—whatever that "it" is that you are wanting to do but resisting.

A resume for your career shows the evidence of your experience and accomplishments. The goal of a Change Resume is to show your experience and accomplishments related to changes that you either initiated or overcame. The goal is to provide evidence to yourself that:

- Yes, you can do it, and you know this because you've done it before.

- Almost every single situation in your life in which you had to endure some form of change, especially the ones you were afraid of, ended up being okay in the end. Either something good came from them, eventually, or you learned something valuable.

By practicing finding the silver lining in what has happened in your life, you show yourself that if what you're trying to do doesn't go the way you want to, something good will come of it because you will CHOOSE to find the good.

Sometimes life's greatest blessings are hidden with life's curses.

> *"Everything will be okay in the end. If it's not okay, it's not the end."* — *Attributed to John Lennon*

The Change Resume activity asks you to look at different areas of your life and identify changes you have experienced. The goal is to identify the positive outcome that came from each.

There are 3 types of changes that you'll be identifying:

1. **Changes that Happened "to You" that You Overcame:** List any circumstances in your life in which an unexpected change "happened" to you, and you didn't see how it was going to end well, but that ultimately in the end you either figured it our or it turned out better than you thought.

2. **Unwanted or "Bad" Changes:** List any negative circumstances in your life that in the end lead to a beneficial outcome, such as a better situation or learning an important lesson.

3. **Changes You Initiated Yourself (or Accomplished):** List any changes you've made or goals you've met that you did by your own choosing.

How to Complete the Change Resume Activity:

1. For each life area, identify important life changes that took place in your life.
2. Identify the "type" of change each incident was (from the 3 options above). Write 1, 2 or 3 next to each event.
3. Describe the situation or change, briefly.
4. Identify anything good that happened as a result, whether it eventually lead to something positive or if you learned something valuable.

Example: **Life Area: Education**

(Education examples could include: changing schools, overcoming a fear, improving a grade, making an impact, changing friends, etc.)

Type: 1

Change: Transferred to a new school, 1980, 3rd grade

Positive Outcome: Met my best friend

Example: **Life Area: Family Life**

(Family Life examples could include: changes from any point in your childhood, such as: moving, breaking an arm, joining a club, learning an instrument, parents divorcing, or getting your first job, car, or boy/girlfriend, etc.)

Type: 3

Change: Joined the t-ball team, 5th grade

Positive Outcome: Learned how to get along with other kids

Example: **Life Area: Work Life**

Work Life examples could include: getting a new job, getting fired, starting a business, changing careers, going back to school, etc.)

Type: 2

Change: Got fired from Bank of America, 1999

Positive Outcome: Ended up discovering a new career path I loved.

Example: **Life Area: Adult Life**

(This could be going to college, breaking up or starting a relationship, getting married, moving, facing a fear, trying something new, learning something new, losing a loved one, divorce, a car accident, etc.)

Type: 3

Change: Faced my fear of heights by climbing the Statue of Liberty

Positive Outcome: Enjoyed the view, even though it was terrifying, and realized that I can handle my fear

Life Area	Type (1, 2, 3)	Situations/Changes	Positive Outcome
EDUCATION			
FAMILY LIFE			

Life Area	Type (1, 2, 3)	Situations/Changes	Positive Outcome
WORK LIFE			
ADULT LIFE			

2: QUALITY VS SAFE PROBLEMS

There are two types of problems in life: quality problems and safe problems. A safe problem is an issue that lingers and affects our life but the solution is within our control. Some example of safe problems are:

- Communication problems or bickering
- Procrastination
- Blaming Others
- Addictions
- Avoiding making decisions
- Time management issues

A quality problem is a problem that, if changed, would significantly affect our identity, environment, or quality of life. Some example of quality problems are:

- Moving to a new area
- Career Change
- Committing to a Relationship
- Leaving a Relationship
- Starting a Family

As you can see quality problems can significantly change our life and even our identity. However, we choose to keep the "safe" problem around as a way of avoiding dealing with the quality problem. This is because quality problems have high perceived risk, while safe problems carry low perceived risk, even though they can destroy our life and emotional state over time. For example, anger is a lot easier to express than sadness because we feel empowered by anger and sadness makes us vulnerable. We may continue to find things to be angry about (safe problems) rather than deal with what's causing the sadness (the quality problem).

As you can see many times we hold on to safe problems because it gives us an excuse not to deal with what is scary and what may produce a lot of uncertainty in our life. However, what holds everyone back from creating the life that they truly want are safe problems. The interesting part is that safe problems are things that we truly DO have control over. For example, we have dealt with clients that wanted to change their job and do something that they are more passionate about. However, they present many safe problems as excuses, such as lack of motivation, procrastination, blaming others, and so on, preventing them from actually taking the steps to changing their career. Why? because the quality problem will create many changes in their life that seem scary.

Uncovering Quality Problems

So, the question is, how do you change this? The first step is identifying the quality problem and the safe problems you use as a way of avoiding the quality problem.

What are some problems you have in your life that you know you COULD do something about, but you don't ever seem to take the steps necessary to change it?

What quality problems—ones that may be harder to change but would dramatically improve your life—are you avoiding?

If you're not sure what the quality problems are, here is an activity to help you dig deeper into the life challenges you're experiencing to find the root.

It starts by asking yourself "why" repeatedly until you get to the core issue and there is no other WHY to answer. When you find yourself feeling frustrated, sad, angry, or otherwise facing an aspect of your life that you're unsatisfied with, ask yourself the following string of questions:

- What is the surface-level conflict or problem that you're experiencing?
- How do you feel?
- Why?
- Why does this bother you or affect you?
- Why do I feel that way about it?

And here are additional questions to ask to discover where the belief came from:

- Are there any benefits from feeling or reacting this way?
- What are they?
- Where or who did I learn it from?
- What benefits did they receive from it?
- Are they right? How do you know?
- What deeper level problem might be going on beneath the surface?

- What does keeping this problem around allow me to avoid?
- Keep probing and asking yourself until you get to the core of the issue.

3: THE POWER OF PAIN AND PLEASURE

Everything we do in life is because we're either avoiding pain or moving toward pleasure.

If you're continuing an unwanted pattern, it's because you're associating more pain to stopping it than you are to continuing it. And if there's a change you keep putting off, it's because you associate more pain to making the change than keeping things the same. The truth is that you KNOW that making the change will pay off and be much more beneficial than staying stuck in old patterns.

Below is an activity that will help you stop unwanted patterns and make needed changes by associating massive pain with keeping around the OLD pattern and massive pleasure with making the desired change.

- What is the PAIN you expect if you make this change? This can be pain from the experience of making the change and/or the pain you would experience if you DID reach your goal?
- What is the PLEASURE you have experienced by NOT making this change? What benefit do you receive from keeping around this old pattern or this problem?
- What is the PAIN that will happen if you DO NOT make this change? How will it impact your life, your career, your family?
- What is the PLEASURE you will experience when do make this change and reach your goals and dreams? How will your life be better? How will you feel? What weight will be lifted? What other important outcomes will come from this?

4: THE POWER OF FORGIVENESS

Breaking down the prison and letting the inmate free is one of the best things you can do to truly create happiness in our life. You may say, "I am not holding anyone in a prison," but in reality everyone creates a prison—and the inmate you are trying to set free is yourself. This prison is created by not forgiving. In fact, many times unforgiveness is the biggest piece of baggage that you can carry. Your baggage could be from a parent, friend, significant other, or coworker—anyone that was not there for you, abused you, took advantage of your trust, or harmed you emotionally.

Often we hold resentments thinking we are somehow getting the other person back; however, they are not affected by our refusal to forgive, we are.

> *"Resentment is like taking poison and expecting someone else to die" — Gautama Buddha*

What is forgiveness?

Forgiveness is releasing the feeling that the other person owes us something…. And freeing ourselves from anger. You may believe that forgiveness is challenging, but when you understand who it is truly for— you—then it becomes easier. When you practice forgiveness you will feel empowered. Forgiveness is freedom.

What forgiveness is NOT:

Many people do not forgive because they have a misperception about what forgiveness truly is. Therefore, let's go over some of the things forgiveness is not.

- Forgiveness is NOT: Reconciliation with the person.
- Forgiveness is NOT: Living in denial about a person's action(s).
- Forgiveness is NOT: Allowing the person to do the same behavior over and over again.
- Forgiveness is NOT: Having no consequence for a behavior.
- Forgiveness is NOT: Having the pain magically go away.

First, Forgive Yourself:

> *"True justice is paying once for each mistake. True injustice is paying more than once. Animals pay once, humans pay thousands of times. Every time we remember we judge ourselves and feel guilt over and over again." — Edgar Cayce*

Many times, in our lives we make mistakes and we have to forgive ourselves for those mistakes. Most people have more resentment toward themselves than anyone else. There are two things that our minds unconsciously do when we feel guilty. One of them is to try to repay or make right our mistake, often excessively. If we feel that there is nothing we can do to make something right, the second option we choose (unconsciously) is to punish ourselves.

Take a moment to reflect on your actions (toward yourself or others) in the past that you may regret.

- Are there any mistakes you made that you continue to beat yourself up for? If so, what?
- How are you punishing yourself for it?
- Are you directly or indirectly punishing others for it?

Your guilt is not going to undo what has happened. Even more importantly, holding onto this pain is causing further pain in your life. It is okay to let it go now. Release yourself from the burden of carrying it with you.

I forgive myself for: _____

Apologize: If any of your self-grievances are towards others, consider expressing an apology through a letter, email, phone call, or in person. (Remember not to be attached to the results since this is about you, not them. Do not expect to be forgiven.)

Next, Forgive Others

Write it down: Make a list of people you need to forgive and what you want to forgive them for. Include what you need to forgive yourself for.

Reflect: Acknowledge the pain that the lack of forgiveness (on your part) has caused you and how it currently impacts your life. Is it more painful than the actual experience?

Learn the lessons: What are some things that you can learn from the situations? Are there any positives that have or can come out of the experiences? What lessons could the other person(s) have learned?

Let go: Release any expectations from anyone else. This includes expectations of forgiveness or apologies from others or changes in others' behaviors. Forgiving doesn't mean accepting unacceptable behavior, but if the person does not change it is your responsibility to free yourself from the pain of resentment and do what's right for you, even if it means cutting ties with the person. What expectations do you release?

Express Forgiveness: ONLY if you feel it would be beneficial to you, consider expressing forgiveness to another through a letter, email, phone call, or in person. (Remember not to be attached to the results since this is about you, not them. Do not expect an apology.)

Live and be free! Forgiveness is about personal power. A life well lived is your best revenge; therefore take your power back and focus on your desires. Don't do it because, "You'll show them," do it because you want to live your life with freedom and happiness. Forgiveness is often an opportunity to learn, grow, and heal. You may even find that the negative experiences were blessings in disguise if you can create a place for forgiveness and acceptance in your heart.

Remember, forgiveness is 100 percent your responsibility. Only you can unlock the door to your prison and shift your life from limitation to freedom and joy.

5: PUTTING THE OXYGEN MASK ON YOURSELF FIRST

Fill Your Cup:

Imagine that each person has a cup. How they feel—their emotional state, health, wellbeing, fulfillment, their energy level—is dependent on how full their cup is. Every person as the ability to pour from their own cup into someone else' by giving of themselves in one way or another. There are some people who are cup-fillers, helpers, givers who go around filling others' cups. There are also people who are like beggars on the street holding out empty cups asking or demanding them to be filled.

Sometimes the givers give too much. Their cups run on empty. They sacrifice themselves for others. They get drained, the feel empty, lethargic, stressed. Eventually they have no more to give. In some cases they become incapacitated or even pass away, leaving behind any number of people who believe they required that person in order to fill their cup.

And this all happens because of one big misunderstanding. Each person is 100% responsible for and capable of filling their own cup. Now, that doesn't mean that people are always taking responsibility for it— many people going around with their cup out looking for handouts.

For the beggars, the good news is that they are more than able to fill their own cups. Often, when dependent people are forced to stop being dependent, a miraculous thing happens—they step up to the plate.

There is good news for the givers too; they can learn how to fill their own cups. There is a better way… no matter who you are, you need to learn to feed yourself, take care of yourself. Do things that bring you joy, utilize your natural talents, or put you in a state of flow. Go for a walk or spend time in nature. For some people, filling their cup is reading a book or playing a game or going to a show or listening to music or creating art. Remember what fills YOUR cup and do more if it! Not only will you no longer feel dependent on anyone else to fill your up, but your cup will run over and you'll have more to give.

The Oxygen Mask:

You know when you're in an airplane and the steward does the demonstration and tells you "in the case of an emergency and a drop in cabin pressure, put your own oxygen mast on first before assisting other passengers." It's cliché but most people miss the point. Have you ever stopped to consider WHY? Because if you don't put the oxygen mask on yourself first, and you lose consciousness, you are unable to help anyone else. In the worst case scenario, both you and the person (such as your child or a partner or a stranger) that you are trying to save will die. It is the same in life. You must honor yourself, care for your own needs, and do what you know in your heart is right for you. If you don't, both you and those you love suffer. It can be hard to give yourself permission to be selfish. Self-sacrifice is a habit with a lot of momentum.

Most of us are taught that selfishness is bad. It's not true. Being willing to be selfish—and take care of yourself so you are at your best and, therefore, are able to bring your best self to the world and those you love—is the most selfless thing you can do.

If you look back at your life you'll see that there are times when you made decisions that truly honored YOU. Times when you did what you loved even if it was unpopular. Times you chose not to participate in something you knew wasn't right for you. Times you gave yourself a reward or took a much needed break. And because you made those decisions, you improved your psychological and emotional state. You became stronger. Your cup became full. And you were better able to care for yourself and others.

- What decisions have you made in the past that honored you? How did they turn out?

- In what ways are you not honoring yourself or taking care of yourself?

- Are there situations in which you are self-sacrificing (or have) to the point of self-harm or no longer being able to help those you are sacrificing for?

- What changes could you make that would help you put on your own oxygen mask on first, so that you're better able to assist others?

- What are some ways you could fill your own cup? What FEEDS you? What makes you feel fulfilled?

- What changes could you make that would stop beggars from being dependent on your filling of their cups?

- If you commit to filling your own cup, how will this change your life?

6: OVERCOMING INDECISION, AUTOPILOT AND BEING STUCK

Indecision is a form of self-abuse. It's the ultimate form of giving away your power because it is our decisions that determine our destiny. One of the most important aspects of life that CBT can help with is decision making.

The first form of indecision is being on autopilot. Some people don't make decisions at all. In fact, they aren't even aware of what they're doing. They blindly follow their impulses, or worse, their familial and cultural assumptions of how life "should" be. Many people respond to the stimulus of their environment with knee-jerk reactions, and their lives unfold on autopilot.

In the most extreme situations, their choices dramatically reduce their options, like choosing to drive recklessly and ending up in an accident that causes permanent disability or accidentally becoming pregnant at 15. Other decisions are more subtle, yet have lasting repercussions. Some people choose to settle for a practical career that they hate or take over the family business out of obligation. They may go to college for a degree they don't want or drop out because they don't know what they want. They may get married, have children, and climb the corporate ladder because it's what they're "supposed" to do. They may fall into habits or patterns that don't serve them or keep experiencing the same dysfunctional relationships over and over again. They may spend hours a day on social media or watching TV instead of working toward their dreams. They never stop to question their decisions and, if they do, it's often only after they're already suffering the consequences. They aren't aware that they could have had a totally different and, most likely, dramatically more epic life.

If you've been living your life on autopilot, this entire book is designed to help you become more aware of your thoughts and behaviors, which means you will be more conscious of the decisions you are, and are not, making. If you've been giving away your power, the exciting thing is now you know that you can take it back. Get in the habit of asking yourself what you want, as well as taking a moment to consider the outcomes or repercussions of the actions you take.

The second form of indecision is being stuck. This happens when you recognize that you have a choice how to live, but you either cannot decide between your options or you cannot get yourself to move forward. You're stuck. There are 4 ways you can get stuck.

1. **Not Sure What You Want:** There may be times you don't take action because you're not sure what you want and so you do nothing. Like so many people, you might reach a decision point and then think and think and think, but never act. But, you are still making a decision because your indecision will ultimately lead to an undesirable outcome. By not deciding, you give away your power. Often, indecision means you wait too long and your choices are no longer available. Other times, it means you allow someone else to make the choice for you. The saddest form of indecision is when you know what you wanted but you let it slip away.

2. **Perfectionism:** One of the things that gets in the way for many people is perfectionism. Don't worry whether it's the "perfect" decision or whether it's the "right" direction. Making any decision in any direction gets things moving. For example, if you got in your car, turned on the GPS, and told it where you wanted to go, it may not initially lead you to the right direction if it does not recognize which way you are facing or if has not updated your location. However, as soon as your car starts moving it will get oriented and then tell you to go in the direction you need to go, even if it means turning around. The same thing happens when you take action in life. Getting started is the hardest part, but once you make a move—any move—it becomes easier to assess if you're going the right way and what steps to take to correct your path.

3. **Being Indecisive:** Are you not sure which option to choose? Try each one out. Taking even one step in one direction or another will help you gauge how you feel about it. If it is not possible to literally take a step or try it out, run through the possibilities in your mind. Imagine making the decision one direction. Imagine taking the first step.

   - From there, what are the possible outcomes?
   - How do I feel about each outcome?
   - For each outcome, what are the possible next steps?
   - Then, make the next decision and ask again…

4. **Feeling Uncertain:** Are you avoiding making a decision to move forward on something because you're not sure how it will turn out? Uncertainty is a big roadblock for many people. It's normal to wish you could know how everything will turn out ahead of time, but the problem is that you can't. The solution is to take a small step. Test the waters. And in many cases, just simply do it!

7: MAKING IRREVOCABLE CHOICES

Living on autopilot or getting stuck in indecision can hold you back and give your power away. Becoming aware of the thought processes that are keeping us from making a clear-minded decision, as well as getting clear about what we want, can help us make better decisions.

But the truth is that some decisions are harder than others.

The third form of indecision happens when the choices are irrevocable, meaning the repercussions of either choice are life changing. Sometimes we're faced with the terrifying reality that when we choose one path it means we will permanently eliminate our other options.

This is why so many people never make a leap into the unknown. They are paralyzed by fear—fear that they'll make the wrong decision. Fear they'll regret what they'll miss out on. They spend so long standing in trepidation that eventually they find themselves living the default life that their environment cultivates. The only difference between them and those who live on autopilot is that they ache inside for the dreams they never chose because they were aware of their options. But, it's too late—the ship has sailed. What they didn't realize is that whether they made that hard decision or not, a decision was made and something was lost. It's inescapable.

Some people run from the truth and avoid pain so much that they miss out on life completely.

When faced with such earth-shaking dilemmas, how do you choose?

- How do you choose whether or not to leave a marriage?
- How do you decide to quit your job and go back to school?
- How do you decide whether the freedom of entrepreneurship is worth the risk and uncertainty?

- How do you decide to move thousands of miles from your family and friends and miss out on important milestones?
- How do you decide whether or not to have a child?

Some life-changing decisions are easier than others.

We have found—through intensive firsthand experience, research into success and happiness, and experiences with our clients—that there are two stages we must go through to make those really hard decisions:

- Honesty
- Acceptance

HONESTY: We must be honest with ourselves about what we will lose, on both sides of our decision.

No matter what choices we make in life, we are destined to have a ghost ship— that contains all of the experiences, people, and options we did not choose. This ship is like an alternative version of our life that lives on without us, floating adrift in an infinite sea. I find this idea to be a great relief. We never have to let something go entirely because part of us holds it in our hearts forever.

The question, then, which of our options do we let sail away?

The following activity will help you really look at the benefits and consequences of each option.

What difficult decision are you facing right now?

What are your 2 choices?

1)

2)

Each of these options represent a life that you will either live, or not. Now, imagine you are choosing to live LIFE #1 and allowing LIFE #2 to drift out to sea.

- What are the positive, meaningful outcomes I'll experience if I choose LIFE #1?

- What are the negative, meaningful losses I'll experience because I did NOT choose LIFE #2?

Now, switch your choice around in your mind, allowing LIFE #1 to drift to sea, and imagine what it would be like.

- What are the positive, meaningful outcomes I'll experience if I choose LIFE #2?

- What are the negative, meaningful losses I'll experience because I do NOT choose LIFE #1?

Put it all on paper. Include everything you can think. Be brutally honest. And when you're ready, really ready to know your answer, sit down and ask the final question.

When you're 85 years old, which one would you regret NOT doing more?

At the end of this exercise, you'll be clear. Devastatingly clear. But that's okay because the weight will be lifted; the decision will be made. And, most importantly, you won't risk letting life pass you by, robbing you of your potential for greatness.

ACCEPTANCE: Next, you must accept the life that is truly yours to live and honor the one you are leaving behind.

You may never know what it was like to live the life you don't choose. It wasn't yours to live. But you'll be able to live the destiny you have created, knowing you made an empowered decision that honored who you truly are. Some of what you've left behind will fade from your mind completely; some will echo in your heart forever.

In order to create our beautiful lives, we have sent many possibilities, people and pieces of ourselves to live upon our ghost ships.

"When I find myself facing another irrevocable choice, I am drawn to the sea. I stand on the shore with the waves lapping my feet. When I look to the horizon, I catch a glimpse of what looks like the shadow of a sail. I wiped away a tear, smile and waved gently to my phantom self and my life that I'll never know, knowing that no matter what I choose, part of me will always be adrift." —Natalie Rivera

Bon voyage.

8: EMPOWERING YOUR VISION OF THE HERO'S JOURNEY

At this point, you are ready to fully move forward. Return to the Hero's Journey activity and reflect on any ways your story has changed. Do you see the story of what already happened to you any differently? Have you progressed further along the journey? What step to you feel you are at now?

This is the moment that the hero does the number one most important act that puts them in control of their destiny. The hero takes control of the pen… that writes the story… They take back their power from anyone that used to try to control their story. They take their power back from any obstacles that may exist, knowing there is always a path around them.

The hero looks at the trail ahead and sits down to write the rest of their story.

Going on Your Vision Quest

And that's exactly what you're going to do now—go on a vision quest. Looking forward at your next steps in the hero's journey and the dreams you have for your life, develop a vision of how your story will unfold.

Allow the steps in the journey to unfold in your mind, like a movie. Imagine what it will look like, feel like, and who will be there at different steps in your path.

Create as much detail in your mind as possible. You can do this with your eyes opened or closed. You can follow the steps in the hero's journey or allow the vision to unfold naturally.

When you get to the end of your quest, pause to really enjoy the moment. Imagine yourself celebrating your success, living authentically as yourself, and sharing your gifts with others. What does it feel like to be the hero of your own life story?

Writing Down Your Vision

After you've imagined your quest unfolding, the next step is to write it down. You can use the hero's journey activity and fill in the steps, or you can write down a summary of what you saw. When writing down your vision, use the following 4 guidelines, called the 4 P's, to help your words speak directly to your unconscious mind in a way that makes your vision believable.

- Present Tense (as if it's happening now, not past or future—no "will" or "ed")
- Personal Perspective ("I" and "me" statements)
- Positive Language (avoid words like "not" or "don't")
- Passionate (put emotion behind it—remember the pain/pleasure)

You can make a visual representation of your vision or keep a copy of what you've create somewhere you can read it daily. As you continue moving forward along your journey, hold the image in your mind of WHO YOU TRULY ARE, standing in your power, determining your destiny with every step you make.

Journey on.

Your Vision:

SECTION 10: CREATING CHANGE–THE PRACTICAL STEPS

1: IDENTIFYING WHAT IT WILL TAKE

Once we've rediscovered our true potential and empowered our beliefs about ourselves and the possibilities of life, we can write the next chapter of our life's story. After everything we've learned about ourselves during this journey of transformation, at some time we need to take what we've discovered and determine what we're going to do with it. What is our goal? What is the dream we are going after and how can we get there?

And this is where people can get stuck. One of the biggest things that holds people back from making changes is not knowing what steps to take.

Often, we can see the big picture vision of what we want, but it can be hard to see how small changes we make today will ever get us there. It can be overwhelming thinking of the journey ahead and everything it will take to transform our lives. We can get stuck in a state of overwhelm and fail to take a step forward. And that's why this section of the program is SO important.

We're going to work on turning that vision into concrete, achievable, meaningful goals. Then we're going to break down those goals into actionable steps.

We will be building a bridge from where we are now to where we want to be.

The first step, of course is getting on the bridge—taking the first step. And the next step is to look at what you need in order to build the rest of the bridge. Then lastly, you will create the plan for completing the voyage.

So, let's start with the first step.

The bridge goes from where you are now all the way to the life where you're living authentically, doing what you love, and being filled with meaning and fulfillment. But, that doesn't mean that those wonderful things only exist on the other side. The key, in fact, to reaching that dream is to LIVE IT at every step of the way. You cannot put off your happiness until this, that, or the other thing happens. You are on a hero's journey. The story is not about the moment the hero accomplishes their mission, it's about the journey itself.

So, when you take the first step, in a way, you're already there. You've already accepted your quest—your quest to become all you came here to be.

What this means is that the first part of your bridge has to contain within it the seeds of what will grow by the time you reach the end. It needs to FEEL like authenticity, love, and meaning. While you may not be able to have everything you dream of in this moment, you can still bring those things INTO this moment.

There are two ways to GET ON THE BRIDGE:

1. Think about the long-term goal you are journeying toward and ask yourself how you can do some aspect of it NOW. For example, if you are going to write a book, you cannot publish your book today, but you CAN write one paragraph. This one paragraph can be your FIRST step onto the bridge. So, what small step can you take today that officially starts you on the journey over the bridge to your dreams?

2. Bring an aspect of your dream into the present moment by LIVING AS IF. Take a moment right now to imagine what it will feel like to be living in that state of authenticity, love, and meaning. The truth is that you can experience the emotions of those experiences Unconditionally—without the condition having to be here. Revel in it, knowing that as you imagine yourself taking that first step onto the bridge you can feel that you are already

there. Reaching the end is inevitable, you only need to keep taking the next step.

Now that you've taken the first step, it's time to start building your bridge. Look back at everything you've done so far throughout the activiies in this book. Below, identify your true desires, the changes that need to be made, and what you've learned along the way. It will be like collecting the building blocks with which you will build your bridge. Then use this list when setting your long-term goals in the upcoming goal setting process.

My True Desires:

Changes I Will Make:

What I've Learned About Myself:

2: SMART GOALS

Not all goals are created equal! Believe it or not there is a science to writing and creating your goals. Knowing how to create goals is one of the major differences between why some people are so affective in reaching their goals and why some are not. In fact, the "smart" goal principles have been popular for quite some time, first appearing in 1981 as presented by George Doran in a business journal. However, the principles behind "smart" goals can be found in books that are over a century old. Success leaves clues, and these goal setting principles have been proven successful. Once you identify what your goal is, compare it to these "smart" goal principles. If they do not meet the criteria, then make the necessary changes. Refer back to these criteria when finalizing your goals.

SMART GOALS are: Specific, Measurable, Achievable, Realistic and Time Framed.

Specific: It is critical that your goals are as specific as possible. Many people set goals that are vague in nature and not precise. The problem with this is that it makes it hard to determine how to get to them and how to judge when we actually achieved them. For example, a statement like "I will lose weight" is too vague. Ask yourself, how will you know with certainty if and when you've reached your goal? In other words, you may reach your goals and still not know that you are there or you may find that you do not have the motivation because you really don't know what you are striving for. Therefore, it would be in your best interest to have the goals say something specific like "I will lose 5 pounds in the next month" At the end of the month or year it will be simple to take a look at your weight and compare it to your goal.

Measurable: As demonstrated in the above example, goals also need to be measurable. For example, if someone is going to school they may say, "I want to be more committed and involved in school" but that may not be measurable. How would you be able to tell the goal has been reached? What is the criteria? This person could instead state clear objectives such as "I will attend every class this month and study for an hour every day." Another goal might be "I will sign up for a student club or organization this week." These goals are simple and concrete. Having goals that are measurable makes it easy for you to track your progress.

Achievable: To build confidence your goals need to be reasonable and achievable. In other words, you do not want to set yourself up for failure, as it will not help you achieve your goals or stay motivated. For example, if a person is trying to write a book they may tell themselves, "I will start and finish the book in two weeks." However, let's say that the person has other responsibilities, such as a job, family, or life; is it reasonable for them to be able to write the whole book in 2 weeks? No. Especially if they've never considered all of the steps it takes. Instead, the person can take a look at their schedule, take all the steps required into account, and say, "I will write the outline for my book this week and dedicate two hours per day for the next 2 weeks. Then I will reassess my schedule and see how much more I have to go." Again, it may be that the person finishes the book in two weeks because they get really inspired or ended up having more time that they initially anticipated. However, it is better to go above and beyond your goal than to make a goal that is not achievable and then have that demotivate you.

Realistic: Another aspect of goals is that it needs to be realistic. With that said, we are big believers in thinking big and stretching reality. However, you do need to understand your capabilities and current abilities when you are making goals. For example, we worked with a senior in high school whose goal is to become a professional basketball player, and he had no other life goals. However, he was not currently playing on a team and had, in fact, never played a competitive sport. He didn't practice very often and was not in the top tier of physical talent or ability. Now, we've also met individuals with their heart set on professional sports that practiced at 4am every day, lived, ate, and breathed their sport, and honed their talent for years. These other individuals were within realistic reach of a goal of pro-ball. However, this other young man was being unrealistic. He was looking only at the fact that he liked basketball and not at what it truly takes to "make it big" in that field. We worked with him to examine other ways that he could be part of the professional league that fit his abilities and preparation and used his knowledge and passion for the game. It is important to honestly evaluate yourself. Do you have the ability? Are you committed to making your goals a reality? Are you doing what it takes? Or can you adjust your goals to make them more realistic? Again, the point here is to build confidence and not set yourself up for failure. But, by all means, if you want to dream bigger and go for the "big time," no matter what that is—then go for it! Just be sure you thoroughly understand everything it takes to be successful.

Time Framed: One of the most important aspects of goals is to have a time frame. Having a set amount of time to achieve the goals gives the mind the structure that it needs to help you achieve them. For example, someone may want to change jobs, start school, or start their own business. However, if they truly look at it they may find that they talk a lot about doing it but never get anything done towards that goal because they have no time frame for it. For any goal to be affective it has to have a sense of urgency. Having a specific time frame give you the motivation needed to get started and finish. For example, for a person that wants to go back to school, they may set a deadline for themselves to register for classes or for financial aid. A person looking to start a business may set a time frame for completing specific research, developing a business plan, and getting the business started.

Remember, there are only two types of goals: the ones that we talk about but never do and the ones that we are truly committed to and will achieve. The difference between them is that the achievable ones are S.M.A.R.T. goals, while the other ones may just be a way of wasting time.

3: SETTING LONG-TERM GOALS

Goal setting is so much a key to success that it's cliché. We know it, but most of us don't do it.

First, we want you to know that this is NOT just another lame goal-setting process. This is the exact process we use to exceed our goals year after year and coach thousands of clients to create BREAKTHROUGHS.

Second, regardless of how cliché it is, setting goals is VITAL if you want any chance of fulfilling your dreams with your career or your personal life.

Most people only consider their goals once per year—around New Year's Eve. And, according to a study published by the University of Scranton, people who don't set goals are missing out because "people who explicitly make resolutions are 10 times more likely to attain their goals than people who don't explicitly make resolutions."

10 times more likely. Those are some good odds! However, your

odds could be much, MUCH greater. What if you could learn what those who succeed at their goals actually DO differently than everybody else... and then DO THAT? Well, you can!

In over a decade of studying human potential and psychology, coaching and training individuals and team members, and running our own businesses—we've learned why most people and businesses fail at achieving their goals.

The truth is that most people don't have the mindset for success.

They don't have goals and they don't make a plan, and when they do, they don't use an effective strategy for executing their plan.

Achieving any life goal requires knowing 3 things, which we refer to as "The 3 D's." In order to know these 3 things, you must ask 3 questions:

- Desire: What do you really want?
- Drive: Why do you want it?
- Do: What do you need to do?

DESIRE: What do you really want?

- ***Step 1: Brainstorm:*** Write down everything you can think of (big or small) that you would like to change, achieve or do. This activity is designed for long-term goals that you want to accomplish within 1 year, however you can apply the same process for longer-term goals or shorter-term goals. When working with goals that will take more than 1 year to implement, you will need to identify which aspects of the goal can be tackled in the first year and focus your attention there. (There is additional space on the following page.)

- *Step 2: Simplify:* Look at your list and group items that are similar or that can be combined into one larger goal. Create a summarized list below:

- *Step 3: Prioritize:* Look at your simplified goals and circle the ones you feel are your highest priority, meaning that either a) they need to be accomplished before other goals in order for the other goals to be possible or b) they are more important to you. Rate each circled goal on a scale of 1 to 3, 1 being the highest priority and 3 being the least. (Write the number next to the circled item.)

- *Step 4: Identify 1 to 2 major goals for this year:* Looking at your priorities, identify 1 to 2 major goals that will make the biggest impact on your life or organization. Always approach the most important goals first. Note that if you are using this process for your organization, you may need to accomplish ALL of the goals you have identified. The execution is more complex, however the same process applies.

  Major Goals:

Step 2: DRIVE: Why do you want it?

When making changes in our lives and working toward larger goals, there are 2 common things that lead us to stop.

1. We get distracted with life. We get busy and encounter roadblocks.
2. We feel uncomfortable with the new change and go back to what we know.

Why do these things happen? Because we didn't have a big enough WHY. We don't have a strong enough drive or motive. Our ability to follow through on implementing lasting change depends on having strong enough reasons to keep us focused and committed through the hard times.

By identifying the true outcomes you're looking for, which are usually how accomplishing the goal will impact your life or make you feel, you will have a stronger motivation because you'll understand why you want the goal.

Look at the major goals you've chosen for the year and ask yourself the following questions (for each goal):

- Why do you want to achieve this goal?

- What is the outcome you believe you will receive by achieving this goal?

- What does this mean to you?

- How will it feel?

- How will it impact your life?

- What will happen if you don't achieve this goal?

Next, we'll get into detail about Step 3: ACTION.

4: CREATING AN ACTION PLAN

Now that you've clearly identified your long-term goals and why they matter, it's time for the final step: creating an action plan.

Step 3: DO: What do you need to do?

Now that you've identified where you want to be in approximately 1 year, you can chart a course to get there.

Monthly Milestones: The next step is to break down each major go into smaller sub-goals. This is called "chunking". Think of your goals as the "big picture" and your sub goals or milestones as the bite-sized achievements that make your goal approachable and less overwhelming. Think about it like working your way backward from the big picture to the small.

- Brainstorm again. For each major goal, considering where you want to be in 12 months, brainstorm all of the things you need to do or have in order to reach that goal. Start by thinking about what would you need to accomplish in 9 months in order to be close to completion in 12 months? Then continue to work backwards to 6 months, and then to 3. Write down everything you can think of.

Brainstorm:

- Then, group items together, with the goal of creating 12 "milestones" or bigger steps, each of which will contain smaller tasks.
- Lastly, put the milestones in order of when they would need to be completed.

Milestone 1:
Milestone 2:
Milestone 3:
Milestone 4:
Milestone 5:
Milestone 6:
Milestone 7:
Milestone 8:
Milestone 9:
Milestone 10:
Milestone 11:
Milestone 12:

You can think of the 12 milestones as coinciding with the 12 months of the year. However, when you are actually implementing your plan, these milestones will not be reached on a month-by-month basis. The truth is, even with the best planning, projects and goals ALWAYS unfold in ways that were NOT according to plan. The goal here is to break down the goal into approximately 12 milestones and identify the order of completion.

Creating a roadmap for your goal and putting it down on paper helps your brain be able to hold the vision of the big picture and the real-life action steps at the same time. This is vital!

60-Day Plan: Now it's time to create your short-term goals. Research shows that anything that is planned more than 60 days in advanced is most likely going to change. Businesses do long-range planning by necessity, but when it comes down to actual execution, you can only plan about 60 days in advance. So, take the goals you determined in the first 2 months of your milestones and break them down further into sub-goals.

- BRAINSTORM: What are the tasks you will need to accomplish in the next 60 days in order to accomplish your milestones? Write down EVERYTHING you can think of.

- PRIORITIZE: Next, arrange them in order of priority and what NEEDS to be done first before moving on to the other things. You can do this by circling all of top priority items within your 60-day list. Specifically, identify the items that need to be completed before other items on the list are able to be dealt with.

1-Month Plan: Take those priority items and put them in a list for month 1 (put the rest in a list for month 2, and save it for later.)

30-day list:

- With your new, prioritized 30-day list, for each item or sub-goal, brainstorm ALL of the TASKS that will need to be accomplished in order to accomplish these sub-goals in 30 days. Write down everything you can think of. Detail is important here because these tasks need to be executable and not leave anything out.

- Prioritize each item on a scale of 1 to 4, 1 being most important OR needs to be done before you can begin on other tasks and 4 being least important or time-sensitive. Write the corresponding numbers next to each task. You now have the next 4 weeks' tasks (1 through 4).

→DON'T STOP HERE←

A small percent of the population sets goals and creates plans that get them to this point. If you get this far, you're ahead of the game. However, most people who reach the point of having a plan for the month still don't accomplish their goals. Why?

WEEKLY PLANNING IS THE #1 MOST IMPORTANT ASPECT OF PLANNING.

Why? Because THIS is where PLANNING meets ACTION. By their very nature, sub-goals in your 30, 60 or yearly plan CANNOT be action items NOW. But, you CAN take actions NOW that will keep you on your path to achieving these milestones.

Without a weekly plan, the week will unfold and no steps toward the goal will be made because existing responsibilities and other's priorities will fill the time.

1-Week Plan: First, Determine WHERE you and any other parties involved are going to put the action list.

- In a daily planner
- On a white board where it can be seen
- In a planning or task app or collaborative task program

Next, Schedule a weekly strategy session. In order to establish the habit of a weekly strategy session, you absolutely MUST SCHEDULE IT IN! Even if you are working on your own, private, goals, choose a time that you will sit down for 20-30 minutes EVERY WEEK to plan the coming week's tasks. If the goal is collaborative, schedule a planning meeting. However, keep it brief and focused on identifying progress and next steps only. Do not include discussions of future milestones or long-term goals in the weekly planning session. Another option is to have your staff complete their own weekly list and submit it to you.

And finally, Write Your "Ta-Da" List

Why do we call it a "ta-da" list? "To-do" sounds like an unpleasant list of tasks that you have to do, while "ta-da" is more inspirational. Every time we finish a task, we cross it off and say "ta-da!" Celebrating even the little victories gives us a sense of accomplishment and builds momentum. We enjoy it so much, in fact, that if we find that we've completed a task that we didn't already have on our list, we ADD IT to the list just so we can cross it off!

Take all the #1 items from your Monthly Plan and write them down as Actionable Tasks. If needed, break tasks down further into sub-tasks.

Identify which tasks are a priority (mark 1 through 3) and plan to do level 1 FIRST or write them down IN PRIORITY ORDER. This is your ta-da list for the week.

Schedule any tasks that are time-framed into your daily planner and assign other tasks to specific days of the week, when required. Keep the rest of your week's list someplace easily accessible to refer to throughout the week when identifying daily goals.

Create Your Daily Plan: Every day, look at what you have on your SCHEDULE as well as your weekly ta-da list. Write in your 3 to 5 sub-goals/tasks for the day and then IGNORE EVERYTHING ELSE.

If you've never tried a goal setting and action planning process like this, you will find that it greatly enhances your productivity and focus! Implemented at a larger scale in an organization, it can be revolutionary.

SECTION 11: THE JOURNEY CONTINUES

1: SYMBOLISM & CEREMONY

Humans communicate in symbols. Symbols are a simple way of expressing a greater meaning. For instance, letters, words and numbers are all symbols. Every culture also has its own sets of symbols that represent different experiences and perceptions that are learned and shared. Great examples of symbols include your country's flag, the cross in the Christian religion, and a heart-shaped emblem that means "love" almost universally.

Symbolism is incredibly powerful to the brain because it cuts through the complexity of language (which itself is a series of symbols) and expresses the core meaning in a way that speaks directly to the unconscious mind. For this reason, using symbolic activities or ceremonies is an ideal way of commemorating important events in one's life. We have common symbolic ceremonies for important life events, such as weddings, graduations, and funerals. By participating in the symbolic experience, the meaning of the event is hard wired into the brain.

When experiencing life transformation, there are often milestones or significant moments that should be acknowledged. Acknowledging these important moments is a powerful way to not only reinforce the changes, but positively reinforce everything it took to get to that point. Some type of symbolic activity or ceremony is a great way to tell the unconscious mind that this transformation is official, real. At the same time, a ceremony can be used in advance of accomplishing the desired outcome, as a commitment to the process or a release of the past.

A symbolic ceremony can be conducted in person or in the imagination. Here are two examples:

- **Burning Ceremony:** Print or write either the accomplished goal or the old belief, behavior, or past activity that is being acknowledged and released. Read it, thank it for its role in serving to help you become the person you are today. Then burn it safely in a firepit, a can, or a patch of dirt. While it burns, celebrate that it is being released.

- **Visualization:** Close your eyes, take 3 deep breaths, and bring into your mind the story or images that represent what is being acknowledged and released, almost as if you're watching a movie. Then imagine turning off the movie, putting the film screen or DVD it is on into a small sail boat, and sending it off to sea. As you watch it gently drift away, acknowledge that you are releasing it and letting it go.

There are many other ways to create some form of symbolic ceremony to signify important milestones, life changes, accomplishments, or the release of something that is not serving you. You can write a letter to yourself, burn an item that represents the situation, tie a note to a rock and sink it, release balloons, release a floating lantern, gather a group of people and make public declaration, giving yourself a symbolic gift, and the list goes on.

We'll leave you with a final example of a powerful ceremony that could be used either in person or using the imagination.

We once heard of a tribal ceremony that illustrates the importance of recognizing that the story we tell about our problems is just a story. This can be the victim story we keep telling about what happened to us in our past or the story of limitations we tell regarding why we can't go for our dreams.

In this tribe, when a community member has a problem, a grievance, or a complaint the entire tribe comes together to support this person.

The tribe gathers in a circle and the person with the sob story stands in the center. He or she is asked to tell their story 3 times. The first two times, the tribe encircling the individual responds with words and gestures of affirmation and support. Even hugs! They acknowledge the story and show empathy for how the person feels.

However, after the 3rd telling of the story, the entire tribe remains silent and turns their backs away from the individual at the center. This turning away signifies their acknowledgement that the story has already been told, and now it is time to move on. The individual in the center of the ring is forbidden to speak of it again.

We honor you for your willingness to reach for the higher ideals of human potential, life purpose, and transformation. We recognize that it can be challenging to face your truth and that it the transformation doesn't happen overnight. But more than anything we hope that you honor and celebrate success every step of the way.

TAKE THE
ONLINE
COURSE!

Learn directly from instructors Joeel & Natalie!

The Complete Guide to Total Transformation online course covers the content in this book through video lectures and printable worksheets that bring the content in this book to life! This a great, fun way to review and learn the material!

ENROLL FOR FREE!
Visit: www.transformationacademy.com/transformationbook/
Use coupon code: *transformationbook*

If you are a life coach (or want to be), enroll in the **Transformation Life Coach CERTIFICATION** program, which includes all content covered in this book, plus additional training for how to use these tools and processes with clients!

UPGRADE FOR ONLY $97!
(That's 50% off!)
Visit: www.transformationacademy.com/transformationbook/
Use coupon code: *transformationcoach*

PLUS, **save 50%** on all of our 60+ other courses!

Use coupon code:
transformationbook50

MEET THE AUTHORS:

Joeel & Natalie Rivera

Joeel and Natalie Rivera are freedom junkies and prolific content creators who have launched over a dozen business. They have also been coaching, speaking, writing, and teaching for more than a decade.

Through their online education company Transformation Academy, they empower life coaches, INDIEpreneurs and transformation junkies to create a purpose-driven life and business and master the power of their mind so they can create their destiny.

Joeel is a former psychology professor with a Master's Degree in Counseling and Education and has been studying happiness for his dissertation for a Ph.D. in Psychology.

After almost losing it all in 2014 due to a sudden illness after traveling overseas, they converted their workshops, coaching and training programs into online courses. Today, they've created more than 75 online courses, taken by more than 200,000 students from 195 countries (at the time of this writing).

They believe that entrepreneurship is the ultimate form of empowerment. They believe in turning pain into purpose. And, they believe in the democratization of education and, therefore, make their programs available at a price that is within reach of students worldwide.

WWW.TRANSFORMATIONACADEMY.COM

Made in United States
Orlando, FL
02 April 2022

16419008R00089